CUSTOM, LAW,
AND MORALITY
Conflict and Continuity
in Social Behavior

Burton M. Leiser received his B.A. from the University of Chicago. After entering upon a study of religion and the Talmud, he received a Master's degree in Hebrew literature in 1956 from Yeshiva University. He holds a Ph.D. in philosophy from Brown University and is now Associate Professor of Philosophy at the State University College at Buffalo. His scholarly publications include articles on philosophy, biblical criticism, archaeology, and religion.

CUSTOM, LAW, AND MORALITY

Conflict and Continuity in Social Behavior

BURTON M. LEISER

Anchor Books
Doubleday & Company, Inc.
Garden City, New York
1969

The Anchor Books edition is the first publication
of CUSTOM, LAW, AND MORALITY *Conflict
and Continuity in Social Behavior*

Anchor Books edition: 1969

Library of Congress Catalog Card Number 69–15213
Copyright © 1969 by Burton M. Leiser
All Rights Reserved
Printed in the United States of America
First Edition

TO BOBBIE

Acknowledgments

Since space, time, and custom limit expressions of thanks to those whose contributions are direct and immediate, many persons to whom I owe a great debt of gratitude must go unmentioned here, but they have not been forgotten.

John Ladd, Professor of Philosophy at Brown University, shared with me his enormous store of knowledge in the area of legal and political philosophy, and directed me to many important sources. His criticisms of the initial drafts of the manuscript that ultimately became this book were most helpful.

I am very grateful to Professor Vincent Tomas, Chairman of the Department of Philosophy at Brown, for his invaluable help, advice, and encouragement.

Professor Russell C. Vannoy, of the Department of Philosophy at the State University College at Buffalo, read the entire manuscript with great care, pointed out several weak spots to me, and helped me to solve a number of perplexing problems.

Miss Lisa Johnson, who edited the manuscript for Anchor Books, patiently and painstakingly examined every word, and helped me to clarify several passages that might otherwise have been obscure.

I am particularly grateful to Ellen, Shoshana, David, Susan, and Illana for their assistance in the compilation of the Index and for the many other ways in which they contributed to the writing of this book, and to Bobbie, to whom it is dedicated.

Contents

CUSTOM, LAW,
AND MORALITY
Conflict and Continuity
in Social Behavior

Introduction

Of the great triumvirate—morals, law, and custom—
only one has suffered virtually complete neglect at the
hands of philosophers. Moral philosophers have studied
morals, they have made an infinite number of pains-
taking investigations into every nuance of moral language, they have studied all the relations between rights
and duties, between actions and values, between the right
and the good; they have populated the literature with
a plethora of theories and commentaries on an infinite
variety of moral issues. Legal philosophers have studied
law, and though they have done less than moral philosophers—particularly in recent times—they too have
made thorough and enlightening studies of legal terms—
of law, right, liberty, duty, sanction, and the like; they
too have developed full-blown theories, of natural law,
positive law, legal realism, and others; and they too have
studied the relations between the various aspects of legal
language. But until now, there has been no philosopher of
custom, and very little has been written on custom and
its relations to law and to morals. Although a few feeble
and superficial attempts have been made to analyze the
concept and to place it into proper perspective vis-à-vis
law and morals, no thoroughgoing effort has been made

since the early seventeenth century (and even that might as well have been written in the fourteenth century, from its scholastic tone).[1]

It might be argued that custom, after all, is a relatively minor concern of philosophers because it is of relatively minor importance. But it will become evident in the sequel that custom is in fact of very great importance, both in law and in morals.

At the beginning of his portion of the discussion on the nature of justice in Plato's *Gorgias,* Callicles distinguishes between what is beautiful by nature and what is beautiful by convention. By nature, he says, it is worse (and therefore uglier) to suffer injustice than it is to do it, but convention declares the converse to be true. He goes on to explain that laws and conventions are made by inferior men in order to frighten superior men into submission, but "nature herself reveals it to be only just and proper that the better man should lord it over his inferiors."

This is only one example among many that might be cited of Plato's concern over the important distinction between nature and convention and the value conflicts that arise as a result of that distinction. Thus, for example, Thrasymachus raises similar questions in the *Republic,* as do Glaucon and Adeimantus. In Book X of the *Laws,* Plato considers once again whether morality is a "mere convention," and adds also the question whether religion is true by nature or merely by convention:

> These people would say that the Gods exist not by nature, but by art, and by the laws of states, which are different in different places, according to the agreement of those who make them; and that the honourable is one thing by nature and another thing by law, and that the principles of justice have no existence at all in nature, but that mankind are always disputing about them and altering them; and that the alterations

[1] I am referring here particularly to Francisco Suárez's analysis, which is discussed in detail below.

which are made by art and by law have no basis in nature, but are of authority for the moment and at the time at which they are made.[2]

Yet another controversy whose crux is the distinction between nature and convention is considered by Plato in the *Cratylus*. Although the dispute there, which is concerned with the question whether names are merely conventional and arbitrary or are in some sense naturally suited or unsuited to their referents, may seem to be remote from the moral and religious questions referred to above, it is in fact closely related; for in the one case we are concerned with the application of such terms as "right" and "wrong" to actions, to law, and the like, while in the other we are concerned with the application of the very same terms to names. If nothing else, the latter inquiry should serve at least as an instructive analogy for the use of these terms in legal, moral, and religious contexts.

Plato, then, and Heraclitus, the Sophists, and other pre-Socratics, were exercised over the distinction between custom and law, and considered it to be a fundamental philosophical issue—or, to be more precise, a family of related philosophical issues.

They ask: To what extent are the meanings of such terms as "right," "ought," "good," "duty," "justice," and the like determined by custom, to what extent by deliberate invention (another form of convention which in certain contexts is called "legislation"), and to what extent are they fixed by the nature of things? Or, to move away from this purely linguistic formulation of the question to a set of questions regarded by many as more substantive: What makes a given act or law good, right, just, obligatory, or their opposites? What is the nature of a good or just legal system, or society, or way of life?

Protagoras replied to such questions with his famous aphorism, "Man is the measure of all things: of that which is that it is, and of that which is not that it is not."

[2] Plato, *Laws,* X, 889D–890A. Jowett's translation.

More than once Plato interpreted this as a relativistic approach to morals and to justice, as for example in the *Theaetetus,* where he has Protagoras say that "whatever appears to a state to be just and fair, so long as it is regarded as such, is just and fair to it."[3]

Philosophers continue to ask the same questions today.

Philosophers of law have generally been aware of the importance of custom to their studies, as anyone can learn from studying their works. It is almost impossible to find a book in this field which fails to mention that custom is a source of law. This mention is usually found in the Introduction or in the first chapter, and with that the discussion ends. There is no analysis of "custom," and usually no explanation of what is meant by "source of law." One is reminded of Hegel, who mentioned the philosophies of the Arabs and the Jews in the Introduction to his major work on the history of philosophy; he considered them to be so unimportant that they are not mentioned again. Hegel was at least quite clear about what he considered to be important and what unimportant, and he acted accordingly by relegating the unimportant to a footnote. Much as we may disagree with his value judgment today, he was at least quite explicit about it. But moral and legal philosophers are quite explicit, and in some instances even insistent upon the importance of custom to their fields—yet they relegate discussion of it to a footnote.

There is a gap in our philosophical studies of social norms, which I shall endeavor to close. For if we are to understand the nature of morals and laws, it is essential for us to concentrate first on the nature of custom and its place among human practices. We must understand the distinctions between customs, laws, and moral prescriptions, and be able to place them all into a suitable theoretical framework.

What, then, are the defining characteristics of a custom as opposed to a law or a moral prescription? Under what conditions does an act become one or the other?

---

[3] *Theaetetus,* 167C.

How frequently must it be performed, for example, by whom, for how long a period of time, and with what intentions? What kinds of sanctions attach to the performance or breach of customs as opposed to legal sanctions? Is a specific legislative act necessary to transform a custom into law? If a law is on the books and falls into desuetude, under what conditions (if any) does it cease to be a law?

Connected with these questions is a host of normative questions. For example, when the populace has built up a system of expectations based upon long-established customs which are opposed to the legal norms, what are the obligations of the state? Under what conditions must it enforce the written law in the face of possible harm such enforcement might bring upon persons who have come to rely upon long-established usage?

Natural-law theorists have long maintained that any so-called law which is inconsistent with the natural law is really no law at all. Must they also hold that any so-called custom which runs counter to natural law is not a custom? Can customs be just and unjust, fair and unfair, good and evil? To what extent do the customs of a given society determine the values of the people who live in that society? To what extent are they determined by those values?

In the realm of law, some people have said that where there are no organized sanctions, or where there is no sovereign to give commands, there can (logically) be no law. Are such conditions necessary for the existence of custom? If not, might the system generally called "international law" be more fruitfully considered as strictly a species of custom? If we were to draw such a conclusion, what practical and theoretical consequences might ensue?

These, then, are some of the questions to which I shall direct my attention in the pages of this study, questions which have thus far received no more than summary and cursory treatment at the hands of moral and legal philosophers.

Chapter I

What Is Custom?

THE APPROACH TO THE PROBLEM

A brief examination of the uses of the word "custom" reveals that it is not univocal. By studying a number of statements in which "custom" and its derivatives are used, approaching the problem through what ordinary-language philosophers call the "paradigm case" method, we find instead that "custom" is used to cover a cluster of concepts, or that it has what Ludwig Wittgenstein called a "family of meanings."

In a famous passage in *Philosophical Investigations*, Wittgenstein says that certain concepts have "blurred edges," and that just as it is a hopeless task to draw a sharp picture corresponding to a blurred one, so also must it be a hopeless task to find definitions corresponding to our concepts in aesthetics and ethics.[1] Indeed, he asks, "Is it even always an advantage to replace an indistinct picture by a sharp one? Isn't the indistinct one often exactly what we need?"[2] In short, must we not finally come to recognize that "the word must have a *family* of meanings."[3]

[1] Ludwig Wittgenstein, *Philosophical Investigations*, tr. G. E. M. Anscome (Oxford: Basil Blackwell, 1958), 36.
[2] Ibid., 34.
[3] Ibid., 36.

This approach has been enormously fruitful in a number of fields in recent philosophy. Time after time philosophers have found that ancient philosophical puzzles have been solved when the confusions caused by over-precise definitions of concepts whose edges are more properly blurred were exposed for what they were. No doubt many of those definitions served very useful purposes; but many of them, because of their artificiality and because of the violence they did to linguistic usages, have tended to confuse and obscure what might otherwise have been relatively clear.

Morris Weitz, in his Wittgensteinian repudiation of aesthetic theory,[4] asserted that the "contention that 'art' is amenable to real or any kind of true definition is false." Art, he said, "has no set of necessary and sufficient properties, hence a theory of it is logically impossible and not merely factually difficult. Esthetic theory tries to define what cannot be defined in its requisite sense."[5] But he goes on to insist that these logical confusions do not render aesthetic theory meaningless or worthless. Instead, he sees its role as being "of the greatest importance to our understanding of the arts." Taken literally, he says, they all fail; but if they are taken "as serious and argued-for recommendations to concentrate on certain criteria of excellence in art, . . . debates over emotional depth, profound truths, natural beauty, exactitude, freshness of treatment, and so on," then aesthetic theory is very valuable indeed.

Recent work in ethics, political philosophy, and the philosophy of law has made use of the ordinary-language approach, and has been very fruitful in clearing up old muddles and in finding the solutions—or at least some plausible solutions—to ancient puzzles. Examples are not

[4] "The Role of Theory in Esthetics," *The Journal of Aesthetics and Art Criticism,* Vol. XV (1956). Reprinted in Melvin Rader, *A Modern Book of Esthetics,* Third Ed. (New York: Holt, Rinehart & Winston, 1961).
[5] Ibid., in Rader, 200f.

hard to find: P. H. Nowell-Smith's *Ethics,* T. D. Weldon's *The Language of Politics,* and A. J. Ayer's illuminating article "The Principle of Utility," in the volume *Jeremy Bentham and the Law,* come to mind immediately, as do H. L. A. Hart's *The Concept of Law,* R. M. Hare's *The Language of Morals,* and Kurt Baier's *The Moral Point of View,* all of which are indebted, to some degree at least, to the approach fostered by Wittgenstein and carried on at Oxford and elsewhere.

In his book, Baier distinguishes between several kinds of rules: regulations, mores, maxims or principles, canons, regularities or uniformities, constitutive rules, laws, and customs.[6] Some of these distinctions, and the criteria Baier uses to make them, are very useful. Others, as will be seen, do not do justice to the variety of our language or to the practice themselves.

If the problems posed in the Introduction to this study are to be solved, perhaps it should first be determined whether "custom" is one of those words that has a family of meanings. If it is, though it may have blurred edges itself, perhaps the interests of clarity will be served if we can distinguish at least some of the members of the family from one another. Once that has been achieved, we will perhaps find that we have gone a long way toward sweeping away some ancient confusions.

Let us begin, then, by setting forth a number of sentences in which "custom" or "customary" seem to be appropriately used. Certain other terms which seem to fit the various uses of the principal terms will be noted along the way. These may be called the "members" of the family.

[6] Kurt Baier, *The Moral Point of View* (Ithaca: Cornell University Press, 1958), Chapter 4.

TYPICAL SENTENCES USING "CUSTOM"
AND TYPES OF CUSTOM

(Note: For the sake of uniformity and linguistic facility each of the following sentences has a similar form. In the analysis that follows, they will be cast into somewhat different forms.)

1. It is customary for Jones to scratch his nose when he's under stress.

2. It was Kahn's custom to pass by this corner at seven o'clock each morning.

> Examples 1 and 2 are instances of habits. Two may also be called a "routine."

3. It is Smith's custom always to give alms to beggars.

> Three may be a habit, but it may also be a maxim or principle that Smith has adopted, always to give alms to beggars.

4. It is customary for the school board to meet every fourth Wednesday.

> Assuming that no superior body has ordered the school board to meet according to this particular schedule, but that it has simply chosen to do so with no particular reason for adopting this schedule rather than some other one, we shall call this a "practice."

5. It is customary for the speaker to address the chair.

6. It is customary for the minutes to be read as the first order of business.

7. It is customary for the Queen's Guards to present arms at the changing of the guard.

> These are examples of standing orders or regulations. They might also be called "procedural rules," at least in most cases. Six and 7 might also be called "routines."

8. It is customary to place a comma after each member of an enumerative series: a, b, c, d, and n.

9. It is customary for Southern Negroes to speak in a particular dialect, e.g., "Is you gemmun [gentlemen] fum de Sout'?"—running syllables together, omitting certain phonemes that are audible in "standard" English, converting "th" sounds (of standard English) to "d" or "t" sounds, etc.

> Eight and 9 are examples of style or linguistic usage.

10. It is customary for the fork to be placed to the left of the plate.

11. It is customary for men and boys to rise when ladies walk into the room.

> Ten and 11 are rules of etiquette, good manners, good breeding.

12. It is customary to rise when the ark at the front of a synagogue is open.

13. It is customary for Catholics to kneel as they say their prayers.

> Twelve and 13 are examples of rites or rituals, or parts thereof.

14. It is customary for the rook to move along the horizontals and verticals only, never along the diagonals.

15. It is customary for wills to be witnessed by two persons.

> Fourteen and 15 are constitutive rules.

16. It is customary in the South for Negro men to call white men "Sir," "Boss," or "Cap'n" when speaking to them, and for the latter to call the former by their first names or by the epithet "Boy."

> I shall call 16 an instance of simple custom, though it might also be called a practice or a convention.

17. It is customary for unarmed fishing smacks to be exempt from capture as prizes of war.

> Seventeen is an example of a rule of customary international law.

18. It is customary in Colorado for murderers to be executed by exposure to poisonous gas, and in France by beheading.

> Eighteen is an example of criminal law.

19. It is customary for dogs to have licenses.

Nineteen is an example of civil law.

20. It is customary for men not to sleep with other men's wives.

21. It is customary for men not to marry within their own clan.

22. It is customary for people not to break their promises.

Twenty, 21, and 22 are examples of moral rules.

This catalogue of types of customs, or uses of the term and the parallel expression "It is customary that . . . ," is not intended to be exhaustive.

Any of these usages of the word "customary" is proper in ordinary English. None of them would sound at all strange to anyone who had not already decided to accept some limitation upon the application of the word. For example, some people might be inclined to deny that 20 and 21 are proper usages of the term, since laws are supposedly endowed with formal sanctions, while customs are not. Although it might be useful to adopt such a restriction, it would seem arbitrary, or at least premature, to accept it at this stage of our discussion. It is certainly not in accordance with common usage. That this is a technical use of the word is shown by consideration of the following statements:

(A_1) It is not customary for people in our community to do X, since X is required by law.

(B_1) It is customary for people in our community to do X, since X is required by law.

To anyone unsophisticated in the vocabulary of legal philosophy, (A_1) would sound very odd indeed. It would sound, in fact, as though the people in that community were inveterate and determined lawbreakers.

In (B_1) there is no apparent contradiction, though there would be one if custom and law were mutually exclusive. Instead, everyone would understand (B_1) to mean that the people in that community regularly acted in accordance with the law, that X was required by law, and that the people in that community accordingly did X. If "custom" and "law" were mutually exclusive, as "horse" and "fish" are, then (B_1) would be nonsensical. Since (B_1) makes perfectly good sense, it follows that "custom" and "law" are not mutually exclusive, at least not in ordinary usage.[7]

When (B_1) is written as follows, however, we do seem to run into trouble:

(B_2) X is a custom in our community since X is required by law.

This does sound odd for reasons which will be elucidated in a moment. Consider first an alternative formulation of (A_1):

(A_2) X is not a custom in our community, since X is required by law.

(A_2) does not seem, on the face, at least, to be exactly equivalent to (A_1). It is not difficult to see why. We are used (dare I say "accustomed"?) to seeing "custom" and "law" differentiated from one another, so that if a given kind of act is required by law, that act is not called a "custom." Notice how the meaning of (A_1) differs from that of (A_2). If "custom" is defined (loosely) as "a practice not required by law," then (A_2) would be analyzed as follows:

[7] Parallel examples are the following:

"*X* is a horse since *X* is a fish." (Or "*X* is a horse and a fish.")

"*X* is green all over, since *X* is red all over." (Or "*X* is green all over and red all over.")

"Horse" and "fish," "green" and "red" are mutually incompatible predicates. When both members of a mutually incompatible pair are predicated of a single subject, the resulting sentence makes no sense. I have used contraries, the weakest type of incompatible predicates. Though some people maintain that "custom" and "law" are contraries, no one to my knowledge has suggested that they might be contradictories.

Though I am fully aware of the problems associated with this approach, I prefer to leave them aside at this time and state dogmatically that it is useful and for that reason we are justified in using it. To enter into the logical problems involved would lead us very far afield.

($A_{2.1}$) X is required by law in our community.

($A_{2.2}$) ["Custom" and "law" have mutually exclusive denotations.]*

($A_{2.3}$) Therefore, X is not a custom in our community.

($A_{2.3}$), then, is true because of a linguistic truth, a fact about the way "custom" and "law" are defined.

Now let us look at (A_1). It seems to be saying the following:

($A_{1.1}$) X is required by law in our community.

($A_{1.2}$) [No acts required by law in our community are regularly practiced.]

($A_{1.3}$) Therefore, X is not regularly practiced in our community.

Notice that ($A_{1.2}$), the suppressed premise in the enthymeme, is a statement of fact about the community, not a statement about linguistic usage. This is significantly different from ($A_{2.2}$). Since one of the meanings of "custom" is "an act regularly practiced," we obtain by substitution in ($A_{1.3}$):

($A_{1.31}$) Therefore, X is not a custom in our community.

The *form* of this statement is identical with that of ($A_{2.3}$), but its meaning is significantly different. For ($A_{2.3}$) means, "If X is practiced in our community, it is required by law," or "Either X is not practiced in our community, or it is required by law," while ($A_{1.31}$) means, "X is not regularly practiced in our community." The formulations of ($A_{1.31}$) and ($A_{2.3}$) are equally legitimate. It is important, however, that we keep clearly in mind their very different significations.

With this in mind, we can return to (B_2):

(B_2) X is a custom in our community since X is required by law.

If the word "custom" in (B_2) is taken to mean "a practice not required by law," then (B_2) is patently contradictory. However, if "custom" is taken to mean "an act regularly practiced," (B_2) is not only not contradictory; it

---

* Suppressed premises are enclosed in brackets. The word "law" in ($A_{2.2}$) is an ellipsis for "act required by law."

makes eminently good sense, and is in fact a completely adequate rendering of (B_1).

If we now take "custom" in (A_2) in the same sense—i.e., as meaning "an act regularly practiced"—we have another version of (A_2) which is identical in meaning with the apparent meaning of (A_1) as outlined above.

Thus, (B_2) and (A_2) are unacceptable translations of (A_1) and (B_1) only if one of a number of possible meanings of the word "custom" is applied. We are strongly inclined, at first, *not* to accept them, because when "custom" is juxtaposed to "law," it is regularly understood to mean, "a practice which is not required by law" (in very general, oversimplified terms). But since there are other common meanings of the term, there seems to be no *prima facie* justification for insisting that only this narrow construction be placed upon the term when it is used in legal contexts. It may be instructive, in fact, to ask why we tend automatically to construe it in its narrower signification in those contexts, though we do not do so in others. This entire question will be discussed later.

Let us proceed now to examine the various types of customs enumerated above, noting both the features they possess in common and those in which they differ. A few general similarities strike one almost immediately. It will be noticed first of all that we are dealing here only with acts, not with mere happenings. In every instance, human agency is necessarily involved. The agent always has the capacity to choose to act in some fashion that is not compatible with the custom, and (if this is indeed another capacity) the capacity to act in accordance with such a choice. This naturally raises the venerable problem of freedom of the will. Since this problem is not our principal concern here, and since it has been effectively dealt with elsewhere, I shall confine myself to a few general remarks. The capacity, or freedom, to which I here refer need not be construed to be contra-causal freedom. It is, rather, the absence of external restraints—such restraints as ropes, chains, drugs, and hypnotic suggestion. In the same category I would include other such physical incapacities as paralysis, spastic twitches and flutters, and the like. Finally, I would include such mental incapacities as feeble-mindedness and certain forms of insanity, which render a person incapable of making decisions or of acting upon decisions once they are made. (There are more subtle distinctions which may—and indeed ought—to be drawn, but that is beyond the scope of the present study.) If a person suffers from any of these incapacities or restraints, then he is unable to act voluntarily—or, indeed, to act (in the proper signification of the word) at all. To say, then, that a given event is an instance of the performance of a custom, or that a given class of events is a custom, that event or that class of events must be the voluntary act or acts of a person or group of persons.

This excludes natural regularities from being called customs. It would be an incorrect use of language to say of a given individual that it was his custom to eat, to drink, or to move his bowels. It would be misleading to say that there is a custom among women of giving birth to children, or that it is customary for the members of a certain tribe to have lungs when they are born.

Since every form of custom entails a certain regularity of conduct, those acts which are spontaneous, impulsive, capricious, arbitrary, or original and different are also excluded.

Finally, though it is not clear how long a practice must endure before it can be called a custom in any of the senses we are about to consider, it is clear that practices— whether they are those of individuals or are widespread and practically universal in application—when they are "flashes in the pan," fads, or crazes, cannot be called customs.

Certain "customs" are the practices of single individuals, while others are the practices of organized bodies of persons, or of persons in their capacity as members of a group of persons. There is some cause for confusion here, since the concept of *person* is so vague and ill-defined. There are not only natural persons (i.e., individual human beings), but there are also artificial persons, such as cor-

porations, regulatory agencies, states and nations. It is
sometimes no easy matter to decide whether a given
practice is to be attributed to the artificial person itself—
that is, to the group in its collectivity—or to the individual members, or the officers or agents, of the artificial
person. For the present, however, let us lay this subtlety
aside.

1. Habits

When one says of a given person, M, that he has a habit
X, one means by this the following:

(1) M regularly does X (sometimes under certain specifiable circumstances).

(2) M might choose not to do X, and not do X (under
those circumstances).

(3) M is (usually) not conscious of doing X when he
does it.[8]

(4) When M does X, he does not do it deliberately.

Suppose, for example, that Jones has a habit of scratching his nose whenever he is under stress. Condition (1) is
fulfilled if he does, in fact, regularly scratch his nose when
he is under stress. If Jones's attention were drawn to his
propensity to scratch his nose under such conditions, he
might, by great effort of will, strive to "break himself" of
his habit. This is condition (2). Condition (3) specifies that
he is not usually conscious of scratching his nose when he
does it. I am not prepared to assert that this is a necessary
condition for Jones's having the habit under consideration,
but it does seem to be a universal accompanying characteristic of habits, that one who has a habit is not aware of
the fact that he is indulging it when he indulges it, unless
his attention is drawn to his indulgence by someone else,

---

[8] Certain important but subtle distinctions might be drawn here.
Thus, for example, one ought to distinguish between being
conscious of doing X, being *fully conscious* of doing X, being
aware that one is doing X, *dwelling upon* or *attending to* or
concentrating upon doing X, etc. Interesting as these distinctions
may be, their elucidation would contribute little to our understanding of the subject at hand.

or by some striking circumstances. As I said above, however, I would not argue too strenuously on this point. (4), however, is certainly a necessary condition for a given kind of act's being a certain individual's habit. It is of the essence of a habit that the person who has it performs the acts associated with it without prior deliberation and without a deliberate act of will—automatically, so to speak.

Each of these conditions, except perhaps (3), is necessary. If (1) is lacking, that is, if Jones does not regularly scratch his nose under stressful circumstances, we would have no reason at all for saying that he had the habit of doing so. If (2) were lacking, that is, if he could not, by any effort of will, no matter how strong, prevent himself from scratching his nose, one would wonder whether this was indeed a habit or whether it was a kind of reflex action (or, as in certain kinds of cases, an addiction). Habits admit of degrees. A person may have a strong or a weak habit. The stronger it is, the more difficult it is for him to avoid doing the act to which he has become habituated. (4) is necessary, for if he does the act deliberately each time he does it, it would be denied that he had a habit of doing X. One would seek the reasons for his doing it on each occasion—or at least it would make sense to assume that he *has* reasons (as opposed to there *being* reasons) for doing X on each occasion that he does it. A teen-ager, for example, who deliberately lights up a cigarette whenever he's with adults, striving to give the appearance of maturity, is not a habitual cigarette smoker. It's only after he has smoked for some time, when he unconsciously reaches for his cigarettes, that he is deemed to be a habitual smoker.

But it sounds odd to say, as we did in example (1) above, that it is Jones's custom to scratch his nose whenever he's under stress. It sounds better, for some reason, to say that Jones has a *habit* of scratching his nose when he's under stress.

I would suggest that it sounds odd because both "habit" and "custom" have fuzzy edges. Either of these terms might be used to describe the observed phenomenon of

Jones's regularly scratching his nose when under stress, but the resulting statements have rather different nuances.

To make the point clear, let us consider another example.

(A) Jones has the custom of kissing his wife every night before he goes to bed.

(B) Jones has the habit of kissing his wife every night before he goes to bed.

If (A) is true, we would be inclined to say that Jones deliberately goes out of his way (if necessary) to kiss his wife each night before retiring. We would also be inclined to say that Jones's having this "custom" is a good thing. But if (B) is true, the implication is that Jones is rather flip about the whole thing, that he unconsciously goes through the motions of kissing his wife before turning over to go to sleep. Such "habits" one would be inclined to discourage.

One might make a similar distinction between the person who "has the custom" of drinking a martini before every meal, and the person who "has the habit" of drinking a martini before every meal. The distinction becomes even more marked when these expressions are replaced by "customarily" and "habitually." We still feel that the "customary" act is deliberate and intentional, and easily changed if desired, while the "habitual" act is compulsive, possibly unintentional and not deliberate, possibly even against the subject's will, and changeable, if at all, only with difficulty. There would seem to be a definite "con" connotation adhering to the word "habit."

But this is not the case with all so-called habits. Thus, one may have the "habit" of brushing one's teeth in the morning. This, presumably, is a "good" habit. It's the kind of habit mothers and teachers like to encourage children to develop. But interestingly enough, it does not carry with it the suggestion that it is performed perfunctorily, like the habitual kiss, or that it is performed involuntarily, like the habitual drink, or that it would necessarily be difficult to break. Furthermore, it's the kind of act that one ordinarily does consciously, though not necessarily self-consciously. In fact, the statement that one has the habit of brushing one's teeth in the morning has most of the overtones of the statement that one has the custom of kissing one's wife at night. Similarly, Kahn's custom of passing by a particular corner at seven o'clock each morning can just as easily be called a habit. In this case, it seems to make very little difference whether one calls it a custom or a habit.

If "custom" and "habit" are interchangeable in some cases but not in others, it is safe to assume that they have shifting meanings. As I stated above, "custom" seems to carry with it the presumption that the event being so denominated is a deliberate act. The cases we have considered here do nothing to call this into question. However, it seems that only those habits which do *not* fit the description set forth above can also be called "customs"; the term "custom" could be applied only to those habits (or—to be more cautious—those so-called habits) consisting of deliberate actions regularly, but deliberately and voluntarily, performed.

It would be incorrect, I think, to deny—as one might be tempted to do—that "custom" can properly be applied to such actions. However, if one is searching for precision, one might recommend that "custom" be applied to only one of the many types of actions to which it is in fact applied in ordinary language. The attempt to do this has been made, but the perplexities to which it has led make one wonder whether the enterprise was not misguided. But we will return to that problem later.

2. Maxims or Principles

When one says that a given person, M, has the principle X, or that he acts upon the maxim X, he means that:

(1) M regularly does X under certain specifiable circumstances.

(2) M might choose not to do X, and not do X, under those circumstances.

(3) M is conscious of doing X when he does it.

(4) *M* does *X* deliberately.

(5) *M* believes that he ought to do *X* under those conditions.

Suppose Jones acts upon the maxim, "'Tis better to give than to receive," or the maxim, "Always give alms to beggars," and therefore always gives alms to beggars when he has change in his pocket. If he did not regularly give alms when he had money to give and was approached by a beggar, one could not say that it was his custom to do so. If he could not refrain from giving alms when the occasion arose, if despite all his efforts not to give away his money he did so just the same, it would not be said that he was acting on the maxim or principle, but rather that he was behaving compulsively. If he were not conscious of giving alms when he gave them, or if he gave alms without deliberate intent, one would say that he was acting out of habit, automatically as it were, not that he was acting upon a principle. Finally, if Jones believes that he ought *not* to give alms to beggars, or even if he does not believe that he *ought* to give alms to beggars, then it could not be said that he acts upon the maxim or principle that one ought to give alms to beggars. He might act *as if* he believed the principle, or *just like* a person who does believe in and acts upon the principle; but if he does not really believe the principle, then one would feel constrained to conclude that he is play-acting, or behaving hypocritically, or behaving irrationally.

It ought to be noted here that when it is said that a person (or group) acts *regularly* in a certain way, it does not follow from this that he (or that the group) acts *invariably* in that way. There is always the possibility that a certain number of exceptions will occur. Thus, if the nose-scratcher refrains from scratching his nose when he speaks before a large audience, it does not follow that he is not a habitual nose-scratcher. And if, on occasion, the person who believes that he ought to give alms to beggars turns down a beggar who approaches him, this is not sufficient justification for denying that he customarily gives alms to beggars, or that he generally or regularly acts upon the principle that one ought to give alms to beggars. The meaning of "regular" will be taken up toward the end of this chapter.

One other distinction ought to be mentioned here. If a person acts upon a maxim or principle, it does not necessarily follow that he does so out of ethical or moral motivations. The maxim or principle might be one of prudence only, such as the maxim, "A stitch in time saves nine." Or it might be motivated by other concerns, such as the desire to further research, which leads university administrations to act in accordance with the maxim that their faculty members must either "publish or perish."

3. Practices

The example cited above of a school board's regularly meeting every fourth Wednesday is a practice which is adopted more or less arbitrarily, because it suits the members' convenience, but which does not have the force of a rule (which will be discussed shortly). The board does not meet on the days specified out of habit or unconsciously; nor does it do so because of adherence to some maxim or principle which requires that it do so. It may have chosen a certain time at which regularly to meet because it finds that that practice in general is more conducive to its members' regularly attending its meetings than would otherwise be the case; but that it should meet on the specific days it does meet can in no way be inferred from the principle that one ought to have a specific time to meet if one is to transact business expeditiously. If the board found it more convenient to do so, it might meet on a different evening each month, or every three weeks, or every five, or on the ninth of each month.

A school board is a person in the technical sense of the word as it is used in law and related fields. Treating it as such involves the use of certain "fictions" as Bentham called them, or highly elliptical terms and phrases which must be analyzed in turn. To avoid this problem for the present, let us speak simply of the members M of the school board S. The analysis, then, of the statement, "The members *M* of *S* practice *X*," is as follows:

(1) *M* regularly do *X*.

(2) *M* might choose not to do *X*, and not do *X*.

(3) *M* are conscious of doing *X*.

(4) when *M* do *X*, they do so deliberately.

A single individual may have such a practice. If he did, he would regularly do the act involved, and would do so deliberately and consciously. This, in fact, would describe perfectly Kahn's morning walk and the "habit" or "custom" of brushing one's teeth in the morning.

Such practices differ from maxims in that the persons who engage in them believe that they are not obliged to do so, or at least they do *not* believe that they *are* obliged to do so.

4. Standing Rules, Regulations, Rules of Procedure

These are rules governing the proceedings of organizations, and also the conduct of persons in organizations. To say that it is a regulation of the group *S* that each member *M* do *X* is equivalent to saying the following:

(1) The members M_1, M_2, M_3 . . . M_n of *S* regularly do *X*.

(2) Any member *M* of *S* might choose not to do *X*, and not do *X*.

(3) When *M* does *X*, he is conscious of doing *X*.

(4) When *M* does *X*, he may do so deliberately, but he may not.

(5) If *M* fails to do *X*, *M* is subject to sanctions which may be imposed by *S*.

(6) *M* may be prevented by *S* (or by its authorities) from failing to do *X*.

(7) *S* may permit its members M_1, M_2, M_3 . . . M_n not to do *X* and not impose sanctions upon members who do not do *X*, either for a specified period of time or indefinitely.

This last condition, (7), amounts to the statement that

the organization may suspend or abolish the rule that X is to be performed.

For example, a speaker must be recognized by the chair before he begins to address a meeting of an organization governed by Robert's Rules of Order. If speakers seldom addressed the chair as they rose to speak at meetings of that organization, it could be denied that such was the custom (1). A given speaker might choose not to address the chair, and might in fact not wait until he was recognized before beginning to address the assembly (2). When seeking to be recognized, he would ordinarily do so deliberately and with awareness of what he was doing, as (3) and (4) suggest. If a person were not recognized by the chair, his action might be considered a nullity. For example, if he made a motion without first being recognized, the chair and the assembly might refuse to recognize the motion as having been made. Or if he persistently broke the rule, he might be punished, for example by being reprimanded or censured, or by being removed from the meeting (5). The chair might exercise various prerogatives to prevent him from persistently violating the rule (6). Finally, the group might at any time suspend the rule to enable members to carry on their business less formally for a time; or, if it felt so inclined, it might do away with the rule entirely, running its meetings informally (7).

Like most of the institutional or organizational rules under discussion, it is difficult to distinguish between those that are deliberately propounded and those which are the natural outgrowths of the way people happened to perform the activity in question—the result, one might say, of a kind of natural selection of practices. Like the English common law, many practices were never promulgated as rules or laws. The practices simply came to be accepted and eventually acquired the status of rules. In a later chapter I will have occasion to examine this process in greater detail, but for the present it should suffice to observe that although sometimes such practices are developed consciously and deliberately, they frequently arise quite unconsciously and unintentionally. We are less concerned here with the *origins* of various types of practices than we are with their *characteristics* once they have come into existence. Some philosophers have suggested, for example, that no practice may be considered a *law* unless it is promulgated. But surely if a practice is treated precisely as if it were a law by the courts, it's of little moment to the plaintiff and the defendant to know whether the law has ever been promulgated or not. Since the court treats it just as it would treat any promulgated law, it *is* a law. One might question the *propriety* of the court's actions, and the *justice* of having laws which have never been promulgated. As will be seen later, in certain important senses, they are laws if they are treated as such by the courts.

A further note is required concerning conditions (3) and (4), on consciousness (or awareness) and deliberateness. In some instances, persons will become so habituated to doing *X* that they will no longer be conscious of doing it, or have the need to deliberate before doing it. For them, it has become "second nature" as it were. However, in such instances, if they are asked *why* they do *X*, they will reply that they are *supposed* to do *X*, that *X* is *customary*, that the rules *require* that *X* be done, etc. This is the kind of answer which would be given by a congressman, for example, who had been in Congress for many years and who automatically addressed the chair whenever he rose to speak, if he were asked why he always addressed the chair. Although some individuals may, from time to time or even on a regular basis, observe the practice unconsciously and without deliberation, it seems, nevertheless, that such practices are generally acted upon consciously and deliberately. In actual fact, such habits, if they are ever acquired at all, arise only after long and deliberate practice.

5. Style, Linguistic Usage

With certain exceptions which will be discussed in a moment, linguistic usages are not set by any authorities.

They simply grow in a way which still mystifies even philologists. Like the other kinds of practices we have considered, they are performed regularly, and a person who performs them might choose not to do so and, in fact, not do so. However, at this point all similarities end. First, of course, linguistic usages, like regulations, are not strictly personal matters, but are culturally or group-determined. Also, unlike other types of "custom" thus far considered, it makes no difference whether the person who performs them is conscious of doing so or not, or whether he deliberately chooses to do so or not. Nor does it make any difference whether the person who performs *X* (a given linguistic usage) believes that he is obliged to do *X* or not. He may simply believe that he is *permitted* to do *X*. There may be a sanction for speaking "incorrectly," but there may be none. (Here we must distinguish carefully among the groups under consideration. A child who says, "Hey, let's have de ball!" in his schoolroom may be reprimanded by his teacher, given a low mark in English, and told to say, "May I please have the ball?" Suppose the same child waiting at first base as the pitcher—who has caught a grounder—hesitates. If this child were to inquire politely, "May I please have the ball?" he would be laughed off the field. Proper usage under these circumstances would be closer to "Hey, let's have de ball!" One may suffer certain unpleasant consequences as a result of using a given linguistic form among persons or in circumstances where those forms are deemed inappropriate. But that very same form may be quite appropriate among other persons or with the same persons in other circumstances. Groups are so fluid and ill-defined that it's often difficult to determine just what "correct" usage is.) Only the most extreme and glaring deviations provoke sanctions. Minor deviations are tolerated, and even major deviations elicit no response unless they are persisted in over a long period of time. One may contrast this kind of situation to that obtaining in a parliamentary body, where breach of the rules is not tolerated for long. An even more striking contrast is provided by the rules of law and morals. Here, a single deviation may be visited with the wrath of society. They are regarded as so important, so inviolate, that no latitude at all, or at most a very little latitude, is granted to the offender before sanctions, formal or informal, are brought to bear upon him.

The same general considerations apply to the group's ability to prevent a person from violating the norms of linguistic usage. Aside from certain specialized situations, such as the teacher who orders a child not to use "ain't" in the classroom, one cannot generally prevent another person from using incorrect—or what are deemed to be incorrect—linguistic forms. The classroom situation is of course comparable in many ways to the parliamentary meeting discussed above. Similarly, certain forms of address, such as "Sir" in the Army, can become highly formalized. These, however, are not ordinary linguistic usages, but norms which have come to be enforced by stern sanctions when they are violated. Although the army lieutenant can demand that the enlisted men under him call him "Sir," he cannot order them to use flawless Oxford English.

Finally, the rules of linguistic usage cannot be suspended or abolished, since no one has the authority to suspend or abolish them.[9] Of course, neither does anyone have the power to proclaim these rules. The most one can do is record the actually existing usages and make certain recommendations designed to regularize or simplify current practice, at least among those groups interested in doing so. This is the most the recent editors of Follett's *Modern American Usage,* subtitled *A Guide,* could hope to do: to guide interested persons along the difficult and tortuous paths of American usage; but they were certainly in no position to legislate, either for the American people as a whole or for any class of persons who use the American language.

[9] The situations discussed in the paragraph above are *special* situations, and differ from ordinary usage in this respect, for there is a person in each of these cases (the teacher, the commanding general) who has the authority to change the rule.

If one says, then, that the members M of a given society S have a linguistic usage X, it follows that

(1) The members M_1, M_2, M_3 . . . M_n of S generally practice X.

(2) Any member M of S may choose not to do X, and not do X.

(Although there may be sanctions, they are so uncommon that they may be considered, on the whole, to be irrelevant.)

Most of the statements considered thus far have been treated as objective reports, as descriptions of the way people behave. Some of them might have been treated in a somewhat different way, however: as *recommendations* or *words of advice*. Generally, the implications are the same as those set forth above; but there is at least one important difference. When A says to B, "It is customary to do X here," intending his words to be taken as words of advice, there enters in an element of *normativeness* which is not present in the same statement made (say) by a disinterested anthropologist reporting on his studies of some distant tribe at a meeting of the anthropological society. There is an implication in the normative utterance that one *ought* to do S, or that it is *right* or *proper* (etc.) that one do X.

6; 7. *Rules of Etiquette and Rituals*

Like many of the other types of custom discussed, these may come to be performed unconsciously and not deliberately. A devout person, for example, may repeat a prayer so often that once he utters the first few words, the rest flow out of themselves, as it were, with no effort on his part at all. In fact, he may find that his mind is on something else altogether—on his business affairs, perhaps. What is true of ritual in this connection is equally true of the rules of etiquette. Those who have been brought up in "well-bred" homes give as little thought to pushing their soup spoons from them as they give to speaking their native tongue.

There is a difference, however, between these two types of custom. No one expects a person to direct himself, in a conscious effort, to the performance of a given act in accordance with the rules of etiquette once he has mastered them and they have become "second nature" to him. "Intention" is in no way required for the proper fulfillment of what we might call the "precepts" of etiquette. But "intention" *is* required for the proper performance of the precepts of ritual. If one rises upon the entrance of a lady into the room while thinking what a bore it is to have to do so, or while thinking of one's latest love, he is nevertheless deemed to have fulfilled all the conditions required by that rule of etiquette. But if that same person kneels during a mass while thinking what a bore it is to have to do so, or while thinking about one's latest love, he would *not* be deemed to have fulfilled all the conditions necessary for proper performance of the ritual.[10] I will not attempt to take up here the complicated question of the nature of the intentions required in various types of ritual. The Hebrew word *kavvanah* best expresses what I mean, but I can do no more than give a few hints as to the suggestions it raises in the mind of one who is familiar with it. In performing a religious act, one must direct one's mind (or heart) to his creator, he must concentrate on the meaning and the purpose of his acts, and he must bear in mind not only the simple meanings of the words he utters, but their deeper significance, their implications, and perhaps their mystical qualities as well. To the extent that he fails to have *kavvanah*, he fails to perform the ritual itself. As I have already indicated, various kinds of ritual have different requirements for *kavvanah*: some more, some less. But I think

[10] I would not want to insist that this distinction always holds. One might find on some occasions that a person who goes through the motions without the requisite intention will be deemed to have fulfilled the requirements, to have performed the ritual, but that one who has also had the requisite intentions is deemed to be more praiseworthy. The basic distinction, however, remains, though in a somewhat attenuated form.

it is a universal characteristic of rituals that they require some degree of *kavvanah* for their proper performance.

It must be remembered that we are here concerned with the characteristics of customs as they exist once they have come into being, and not with descriptions of their origin or the means used to perpetuate them. A child learning the rules of etiquette at a finishing school may be told why it is desirable for men to rise when women enter the room, or why it is desirable for them to push rather than pull their spoons. He may be told to concentrate on performing these motions whenever suitable occasions arise. He may even be urged to think of the reasons for the rules as he performs them. But these exhortations are purely pedagogic, the "intentions" functioning merely as mnemonic devices; the latter are in no way intended to remain as a permanent part of the act itself. A manual of etiquette obviously will not exhort its readers to perform the prescribed acts with *kavvanah,* but a religious manual will.

It is also necessary to state at this point that the difficulty an outside observer might have in discovering whether a given individual has the requisite intentions is beside the point. It is fairly easy to make such determinations in some cases, but in others it is very difficult. We are faced with the same problem in criminal law, where intent is deemed necessary for the performance of a criminal act, though it is often very difficult to prove that such intent existed. All the vagaries of the problems raised by behaviorism will not be entered into here. These have been dealt with quite effectively elsewhere, and any attempt to perform the task here would lead us very far afield. Let it suffice to say, rather, that our language does not reflect a behavioristic bias, but makes many subtle and useful distinctions which a purely behavioristic analysis would have to gloss over.

"Rite" and "ritual" are usually, though not always, associated with religious ceremonials, where the importance of intention is fairly obvious. They may appropriately be used with reference to other solemn acts performed in accordance with prescribed rules. However, I think that in most such instances, the rule concerning intention set forth above remains applicable. For example, not too long ago people were wont to talk about the *rites* of courtship. I dare say if any young man had gone through the external motions of showering attentions upon a young lady without the slightest intention of marrying her, we would say, not only that he was cruel and sadistic—and possibly self-serving—but also that he had not really been courting her. We might appropriately say that he had given the *appearance* of courting her, and that he had *deceived* her and others into *believing* that he was courting her; we might say that he had *pretended* to be courting her, or that he had *acted as if* he were courting her; but we would insist that he had not actually been courting her. Other forms of ritual not at all bound up with religion would be patriotic expressions or demonstrations, such as saluting the flag, pledging allegiance, and singing the national anthem.

Still other forms of usage which are sometimes called rituals are more appropriately denominated rules of etiquette, and are in fact listed as such by numerous authorities (such as the compilers of the Oxford English Dictionary); the prescribed ceremonials of courts, the usages of diplomatic intercourse, etc. Rules of etiquette and rituals share in common the following characteristics. From the statement, "X is a rule of etiquette (or a ritual) in society S," one can infer that:

(1) The members of S regularly do X.

(2) Any member M of S might choose not to do X, and not do X.

(3) Any member M of S is subject to sanctions if he fails to do X.

(4) The members (or authorities) of S may (either formally or informally) suspend or abolish the rule that X is to be done.[11]

---

[11] I have been informed by an expert in such matters that certain rules of etiquette are suspended from time to time. Thus, for example, though it is not considered proper for

But they differ significantly in the following two respects. For one thing, it is irrelevant whether a rule of etiquette is performed consciously, whether the person who acts in accordance with its directives does so deliberately or automatically, and even whether he believes that he ought to do *X*. Indeed, he might even believe that he ought *not* to do *X*. Rituals, however, are such that they must be performed consciously, deliberately, and in the belief that (in some sense, at least) they ought to be performed. In the second place, ordinarily a person may not be prevented from committing a breach of etiquette if he expresses a design to do so (though his intention may be greeted by expressions of shock and horror, and he may be *urged* not to do what he has set himself to do). However, in many instances, at least, he may be prevented from committing a breach of ritual law. If a priest, for example, expresses his intention to deviate from the prescribed ritual, he may be expelled from the Church or otherwise prevented from carrying out his intention. Similarly, under some circumstances people may be forced to rise for the national anthem, to pledge allegiance, and the like.

It is perhaps worth pointing out that ritual and etiquette share one more attribute, albeit a negative one: Neither of them need be justified by an appeal to utilitarian considerations. In this respect, they differ from other rules, such as a fisherman's rule of thumb on catching fish. A good fisherman who finds that such a rule is not helpful in his attempts to catch fish will not follow it and will not commend it to others. However, there is still a sense in which rules of etiquette and ceremonial or ritual rules are ends in themselves. They need not be effective in reality for any purpose whatever, though it may be that some

---

guests at dinner to help themselves to salad from a salad bowl, in these days of "poor help," the rule is suspended on most occasions. The presumption seems to be that the rule has not been abrogated or even fallen into perpetual desuetude, but that if the maid problem is alleviated at some time in the future, the proper hostess will once again be expected to have her maids serve the salad to each guest individually.

of them bring about useful results. As for the rules of etiquette, they are observed simply because it is expected by polite society (or whatever the group may be) that they will be. A person may observe them, even if he believes them to be completely otiose, simply in order to avoid the sanctions which will be applied by society if he does not do so. It is usually believed that rituals serve some recondite purpose or other, such as the swaying of God's intentions, or communion with him, or the like. However, it seems that there is no way of verifying the usefulness of such rituals for carrying out their avowed purposes, and in fact, most of the persons who perform them are not really interested in pursuing the question of their efficacy. It is taken as axiomatic that they are efficacious.

8. Constitutive Rules

This kind of rule is different from all others thus far considered in that the activity under consideration is itself determined by the rules involved; without the rules, the activity would not exist. Thus, for example, one could not play the game of chess without first knowing the rules of chess. In this respect chess differs from fishing, for example, or growing tomatoes. If one does not know the rules of chess, one cannot even play the game badly; he cannot play it at all. Getting married, passing sentence, making a will, and entering into an agreement are other examples of such rule-determined activities.

Some rather unique consequences follow from the nature of such activities. Unlike other types of activity so far considered, it is not sufficient to say that when that activity is engaged in, the rule is *regularly* observed. Rather, it must be said that the rules are *always* observed whenever a rule-determined activity is engaged in, since one cannot even participate in the activity in the first place without observing the rule.

One might object to this by noting that people sometimes cheat. They don't always observe the rules. I am constrained to reply, however, that in such cases they aren't really playing the game, they aren't engaging in the activity.[12] Since this is so, an interesting kind of "sanction" always applies to such cases: the sanction of nullity. If we catch a chess player moving his rook along the diagonals, we nullify his move and make him move again. If a wedding is scheduled to take place at noon and everyone is present but the groom, the wedding may not proceed in his absence. If it does, if everyone goes through the motions, no wedding has in fact taken place. If a judge pronounces sentence upon a criminal defendant before the jury has returned its verdict, he has merely gone through the motions of pronouncing sentence; no sentence has in fact been pronounced, since one of the rules determining the pronouncing of sentences requires the prior rendering of a verdict. Similarly, one who signs his will but neglects to have it witnessed has in fact failed to make a will; he thus subjects his "will" to the sanction of nullity.

A typical statement about such a rule-dependent activity will reveal the other implications of such statements:

It is customary (when playing chess) for the rook to move along the horizontals and verticals only, never along the diagonals.

Notice first that the statement is not to the effect that playing chess is a custom. Whether it is or is not is left open. It is only about an activity that regularly (or as we

---

[12] Some rule-determined activities make provisions for rule violations. In football, for example, if a player is off side, his team may be penalized by losing a certain number of yards. But this is not the same as cheating, since the game itself has built into it the possibility that a player may be off side and provides the penalty for it. If a football team is consistently off side, we would not say that its members were cheating or that they were not playing football—though we might wonder about their tactics. But if a chess player consistently moved his rooks along the diagonals, we would have to say either that he was cheating or that he was playing some game other than chess.

have already pointed out, always) takes place when one is playing chess.

For consistency's sake, the statement above may be reworded to conform to the pattern already established:

In society *S* (e.g., the class of persons who play chess), it is the custom for each member *M* to do *X* (e.g., move his rook only along the horizontals and verticals, never along the diagonals).

(1) In *S*, the members *M* regularly—in fact, always—do *X*.

(2) A given member *M* might choose not to do *X*, but he may not fail to do *X* and remain in *S*. (That is, if he moves his rook along the diagonals or in some way other than that prescribed by the rules, he is no longer playing chess.)

(3) *M* is conscious of doing *X*.

(4) *M* does *X* deliberately.

Most rule-determined activities require conscious, deliberate conformance. A bride who has been hypnotized or is under the influence of drugs has good ground for an annulment, even though she may have gone through all the motions of a wedding ceremony. Similarly, a man of unsound mind may not make a will or validly sign a contract. There are difficult cases, such as the computer that "plays" chess. It is not worthwhile to spend time discussing this puzzle here. For what it is worth, however, let me observe that if it makes sense to speak of two players in such a game, the human participant and the computer, then it also makes sense to speak of two players in a game of solitaire: the human participant and the deck of cards.

(5) It is not necessary to assume that *M* believes that he ought to do *X*, since he may very well believe that he should not belong to *S*. However, some people who "play" these "games" believe that *if* they are to play the game, they must observe the rule.

(6) If *M* fails to do *X*, he is subject to the sanction of nullity.

(7) *M* may be prevented from violating *X* by being excluded from *S*.

This is a peculiar sense of the word "prevention." *M* may be prevented from violating *X* by being excluded from *S*—that is, by not being counted among those who participate in the activity in which he wants to participate, or (in other words) by having the sanction of nullification invoked against him. For example, Jones may not be prevented by society from failing to have two witnesses attest to his will; that is, he may not be compelled to have two witnesses sign the document he calls his "will." But he is prevented by society from having such a document treated as a *will*. Or, to put the same thing in another way, if he wants to have a will, he is compelled to have two witnesses sign it. But this kind of compulsion differs radically from the compulsion exercised by the chairman of the parliamentary meeting who prevents a disorderly member from speaking by gaveling him down or having him removed by the sergeant at arms. In this latter case, the compulsion takes the form of physical force; in other similar cases it may take similar or analogous forms. But in the present instance the "compulsion" is a species of logical necessity: He simply cannot (logically) participate in the desired activity unless he conforms to the rules.

(8) This type of rule may be suspended or abolished.

Chess players may find that the game is more interesting if the rooks move along the diagonals, and rule that henceforth they may do so. The legislature may rule that henceforth wills need not be witnessed. Or in a given instance (as during time of war), the rule that bride and groom must be present at the wedding ceremony might be suspended.

9. *Simple Customs*

There is yet another type of custom which has no special name, as far as I can tell. It is exemplified by the requirement that Negroes in the South refer to white men by the titles "Sir," "Boss," or "Cap'n," while white men refer to Negroes by their first names (with certain exceptions).[13] Members of the society involved must abide by such customs on pain of social sanctions—usually informal, but sometimes very severe in nature. It matters little whether the agent is aware of his "duty" under the rule of custom or whether he performs his duty consciously or unconsciously, so long as he conforms. He may even believe that he ought not to conform, that the custom is evil; but as long as the prevailing expectation endures, and power to exact meaningful sanctions remains in the hands of persons who harbor those expectations, the custom will continue to exist. Whether such customs can be suspended or abolished is problematical. It is obvious that they may be overlooked. A white merchant in Mississippi may choose to overlook a Negro's calling him by his first name, for example—or an entire community may do so for a time for a variety of motives (such as the desire to avoid unfavorable publicity). But the custom may continue to exist in the sense that once favorable conditions return, its observance will once again be enforced. In other words, custom may be a kind of dis-

---

[13] Other examples would be the requirement in our society that men wear trousers, the taboo against a mother's nursing her infant in public, the expectation that married couples will not quarrel in public (the custom being that they quarrel at home if they quarrel at all), and the custom that one wash one's hands before eating. Our customary form of greeting is shaking hands, except that exchange of kisses is expected in certain subgroups, and exchange of non-contact kisses in others. (A non-contact kiss is one in which the two people who are greeting one another embrace lightly for a moment, touch cheeks, and with pursed lips smack lightly at the air.) The power of custom was brought home very clearly when I saw a young couple subjected to public scorn and ridicule and eventual ostracism by a large part of the community in which they lived when it became known that because of their religious convictions, neither of them would shake hands with a person of the opposite sex. Of course, it would be easy to cite examples from other cultures, but for our purposes, these examples from our own should suffice.

position which may exist *in potentio* even when not
practiced *in actuo*. *Suspension* requires a deliberate act by
the group or its authorized representative. So does abolition. Since there is no authoritative source of customary
rules of this sort, they can be neither suspended nor
abolished, though they may be overlooked or simply fail
to be observed (that is, fall into desuetude). With this
qualification, then, we say that ordinarily, simple customs
are regularly practiced. Only where custom begins to
shade into morality do we find that society exerts direct
compulsion upon its members, or countenances direct
compulsion by its members to prevent others from violating its customs. Thus, for example, in cases where it is
customary for a man to marry a girl with whom he has
committed fornication, the father of the girl will be permitted to force the man to marry her if he shows signs of
violating the custom.

10. International Law

We are now entering the fuzziest area we have yet
encountered. There are at least two major kinds of international law recognized by experts in the field: customary
and conventional. The latter comes into being by treaties
and other forms of formal international agreement, the
former simply constitutes the practices accepted and recognized by the community of nations, even though such
practices may never have been reduced to writing or been
the subject of conscious acceptance or adoption by any
given nation or indeed any nation at all.

The nations of the world can be looked upon in this
context as persons constituting a community. Like any
other community, they can by common consent adopt
rules which behave much as rules do in municipalities or
in smaller communities. I shall not enter into all the
problems that arise in this area at this time, since this
will be one of the chief areas of concern later in this study.
However, let me enumerate a few of the characteristics
international customary law possesses, using the example

cited earlier—the custom that unarmed fishing smacks are
not to be captured as prizes of war.

This is a classic case that is frequently cited in treatises
on international law. The United States Supreme Court
ordered that the owners of a Spanish fishing smack be
indemnified for the loss of their vessel after it had been
seized and sold by United States forces. It also assessed
damages and costs against the defendant. This was done in
spite of the fact that no formal treaty or convention
existed governing the subject. It relied entirely on immemorial usage, the custom of nations.

Thus, if *S* represents the society or community of nations, *M* is a member nation, and *X* is a rule accepted by
international usage, the following statement might be
made:

"It is customary for each member *M* of *S* to do *X*."

This has the following implications:

(1) The members of *S* regularly do *X*.

(2) Any given member *M* might choose not to do *X*,
and not do *X*.

(3) When any member *M* does *X*, *M* is conscious of
doing *X*.

(4) When *M* does *X*, *M* does so deliberately.

It may seem odd to say of a nation that it does anything
deliberately, or that it is conscious of anything. A detailed
discussion of this difficult subject would lead us far afield.
It will be assumed, therefore, for simplicity's sake, that a
nation's consciousness is identical with that of its policy-
makers.

(5) *M* believes *M* ought to do *X*.

(6) If *M* fails to do *X*, *M* is subject to sanctions.

(7) *M* may be prevented from violating the rule that *X*
is to be done by *M* or by other members of *S*.

The kinds of sanctions that can be imposed upon nations are well known. They include economic boycott,
refusal to sell arms, blockade, and ultimately war. They
may also include the imposition of fines, demand for
apologies, withdrawal of recognition, and other measures.
Similarly, a nation may be prevented from violating a rule

of international law by the threat or actual use of such measures.

(8) *S* may suspend or abolish *X*.

The members of *S* may enter into a convention which effectively alters the existing customary law.

(9) *X* is consistent with, or follows from, the natural law.

I enter this provision here for the first time, not because it might not be applied to other kinds of custom which we have already considered, but because it has been applied so consistently to the particular type of custom now under consideration. By introducing it, I do not intend to prejudge the question, whether condition (9) is indeed necessary, or even whether there is a "natural law" which has applicability to international or any other kind of law. This problem will be taken up in the sequel, with the discussion of the general problems of the nature of law.

Looking back now, let us see what general conclusions can be drawn from what has thus far been said.

THE MEANING OF "REGULARITY"

In every instance so far examined, the event which is said to take place "customarily" occurs with some regularity. But "regular occurrence" is a notoriously vague phrase. How often does an event have to occur before it can be said to occur regularly? Every day? Every hour? Every few months? Every year? It obviously depends on the event in question. The pendulum of a grandfather's clock swings regularly every second, the new moon appears regularly every twenty-ninth day (give or take a little), and Halley's comet approaches the sun regularly every seventy-sixth year. In human affairs, much the same situation prevails. Jones, the habitual nose-scratcher, regularly scratches his nose when he's under tension, and since an hour seldom passes without some tense moment or other, he scratches his nose every hour or so. Mrs. Jones regularly drinks a cup of coffee with her breakfast—once a day, that is. And Mr. Smith regularly sends an anniversary gift to Mrs. Smith—once each year.

When events that take place on a cosmic scale, such as celestial events, are discussed, in addition to their imputation of regularity, more or less precise equations of time are implied—once each second, or every twenty-nine days, or every seventy-six years, etc. With human events, this is not necessarily the case. Few people are like Kant, whose daily walks are alleged to have occurred with the precision of clockwork. Mr. Jones may get tense, but it's unlikely that an observer studying Jones over a long period of time with a stopwatch would be able to come up with a formula by which he could predict the precise moment of Jones's next nose-scratch. Nevertheless, one says that Jones is a habitual nose-scratcher and that he regularly scratches his nose; for "regularity" in this context is not rigidly time-bound.

Ordinarily, one cannot say that a given event occurs regularly if it has happened only once or twice. An event which happens only once or twice does not happen regularly. Thus, for example, if a bolt of lightning strikes the Empire State Building, and no other bolt of lightning ever does, one cannot say that the Empire State Building is regularly struck by lightning; only if it is struck many times can one properly say that it is regularly struck by lightning. Thus, repetition seems to be of the essence of regularity. Notice, incidentally, that here too, the regularity is not dependent in any very important way upon time. There may be a lapse of many months between one lightning-strike and another, or a lapse of only a few hours. Nevertheless, time is still relevant; for if many years should elapse between one strike and another, we would no longer be justified in saying that the building was struck regularly.

In some contexts, "regularity" implies "generality." That is, when we say that X is regularly practiced by the members of Y, we may mean, among other things, that a large proportion of the persons who are members of Y do X. But generality alone is not sufficient to establish regular-

ity in such contexts. Some temporal regularity seems to be
a necessary condition as well. Thus, there are certain
kinds of acts which are practiced by large segments of
populations for relatively short periods of time—fads and
crazes, for example—which cannot properly be called
custom in any sense whatever, simply because their practice has not been sufficiently regular in a temporal sense.

Since every kind of "custom" is characterized by some
kind of regularity, it would follow that any kind of act
which may not be so characterized is not a custom in any
sense whatever. Thus, for example, an impulsive act would
not fall under any of the rubrics set forth above. The
statement, "Jones has the custom (habit, etc.) of shooting
men he finds in bed with his wife," makes no sense if
Jones has never shot anyone, or if he has shot only one
such person. For the same reason, capricious acts, or
those that are performed spontaneously, cannot be called
"customs."

There is another species of behavior, however, which
cannot be called "customary" even though it is characterized by almost perfect regularity in every sense of the
word. "Custom" is always used to describe a species of
act. A *natural regularity* cannot, therefore, be called a
"custom" except in the most extended sense. Thus, for
example, one can call neither the law of gravity nor
man's so-called "obedience" or "adherence" to it a custom.
Nor is the flow of blood through a man's veins a habit.
Even eating and drinking are not customs, though certain
customs may be associated with them (such as the hours
at which one dines, the foods and beverages one consumes,
the manner in which one eats and drinks, and so on). In
general, whenever we lack the physical capacity to behave
otherwise than we do, we cannot call our behavior "customary." Thus, those forms of behavior which are ordinarily beyond our power to control, or only controllable in a
limited sense (such as excretion, the blinking of one's eye-
lids, swallowing, and the like) are not customary in any
sense; nor is it correct to say of a person whose body
makes motions which are out of the ordinary but un-

controllable (such as twitches and spasms) that he has the custom or habit of making such motions.

In some cases, one can appropriately speak of a regularity without even a single instance of the event in question having happened, or with only a single instance of its having happened. Thus, for example, as a new ship starts out on its maiden voyage from London to New York, someone might properly remark, "That ship now sails regularly across the Atlantic." Or the president of the shipping line might announce, prior to the building of the ship, that a new ship will regularly carry passengers between London and New York.

The reason for this is not hard to find. Even in this case, the regularity will not exist unless the ship does actually cross the Atlantic a number of times. The announcement of the line's president is a statement of intent, or the issuance of an order or a rule, not a statement of fact. The witness's remark about the maiden voyage is an elliptical way of making a prediction or of repeating the *rule* that the shipping line has established. If it is intended simply as a statement of fact, it might turn out to be false, just as the prediction might—as it would be if the ship sank on its maiden voyage, in which case it would not have been true that the ship sailed regularly between London and New York.

CUSTOM AND TWO KINDS OF RULES

Every custom is a kind of rule. (It may be recalled that the word "regular" is derived from the Latin *regula*, which means *rule*.) In saying that X happens regularly, one may mean that it happens *as a rule;* that is, that it happens in such way that a general statement can be found such that each occurrence of X can be subsumed under the statement as a particular instance of it, and that from it predictions can be made as to future occurrences of X. Thus, for example, when I say that the

moon regularly reappears as a new moon, I may mean
that there is some general statement (such as "The moon
goes through a cycle of all its phases every twenty-nine
days") such that each reappearance of the moon is a
particular instance of the state of affairs described in the
statement (a phase which occurs each twenty-ninth day);
and from that general statement predictions on the phases
of the moon can be made.

There is another kind of rule, however, which is also
relevant to our discussion, namely, a rule that prescribes
that under certain conditions, one must (or ought to) do
so-and-so. Thus, for example, there is a rule to the effect
that when the light turns red, automobile drivers must
bring their vehicles to a halt. Unlike the first kind of rule
(which tells us how people [or things] actually behave),
this kind of rule "holds" even when many people do not
behave in accordance with the rule. Thus, drivers would
still be under an obligation to stop at red lights even if
many of them failed to do so. The moon is not *under an
obligation* to reappear every twenty-ninth day, nor does
Jones have an obligation to scratch his nose when he's
tense.

The distinction may be expressed simply in terms of
the classical distinction (made by John Stuart Mill and
others) between descriptive laws and normative or prescriptive laws. Regularities (or rules) of the first type are expressions of, or are explained in terms of, descriptive laws;
a statement that such a regularity exists is a statement to
the effect that such-and-such events do as a matter of fact
occur in a certain fashion. Rules of the second type are
expressions concerning rule-*guided* behavior; a statement
that such a rule exists is equivalent to the assertion that
there is a rule by which people govern their behavior in
regard to such-and-such.

An examination of the list of types of "custom" shows
that some fall more readily into one of these categories
and some into the other. Thus, habits are clearly not rule-
guided behavior. When Jones scratches his nose, he is not

doing so because of some rule by which he feels he ought to govern himself. The explanation for his behavior lies, not in a rule by which he chooses to live, but in some quirk in his make-up, some nervous defect, perhaps, which presumably might be discovered by a scientist possessing the necessary equipment and knowledge. The statement that Jones regularly scratches his nose when he is under stress is purely descriptive. Jones's "custom" (if we can call it that) has been completely described once he has stated that whenever he is under stress, he scratches his nose.

Consider now the Southern Negro's "custom" of addressing white men by the titles "Sir," "Boss," or "Cap'n." One might describe a given Negro's behavior and note, among other things, that whenever he addresses a white man, he uses one of these titles. Although such an account would be quite adequate as a pure description of the Negro's behavior, it would be leaving out a very important aspect of his behavior—namely, that it is guided (or in this case we might say *governed*) by a rule, a prescription which demands that he address the white man thus, and prohibits his addressing him in certain other ways.

One might be inclined to suggest that if a complete account of rule-guided behavior must include the fact that there is a rule governing the behavior under consideration, then a complete account of a given habit, for example, ought to include the psychological and physical laws which govern that behavior. The difference, however, lies in the laws or rules; for the former are normative or prescriptive, while the latter are descriptive. Since this distinction has been ably discussed elsewhere, I shall pursue it no further here. There is another distinction, however, which ethnographers use and which ought to be considered briefly.

Suppose an anthropologist, *A*, in studying a given culture, *Y*, is told by an informant, *B*, that the members of *Y* have a certain custom, *X*. Suppose further that *B* is quite authoritative, and that careful checks conclusively demonstrate that the people generally agree that X is obligatory. We would say that X is a rule in Y, which guides the behavior of the members of Y.

Suppose further, however, that A finds that the members of Y do not actually behave in accordance with rule X. Suppose that he finds that in reality, they behave in accordance with some other rule which is in conflict with X. A simple, and typical, example: The members of Y believe that marriage of third cousins is forbidden, but third cousins consistently marry one another.

Now there is a sense in which both of the following seemingly inconsistent statements are true:

(A) It is customary in Y for third cousins not to marry.

(B) It is customary in Y for third cousins to marry.

(A) is true in the sense that there is a rule in Y prohibiting the marriage of third cousins. (B) is true, for third cousins do in fact regularly marry. (A) and (B) can both be true, with no inconsistency, because "customary" is being used in two different senses. It is being used in (A) with reference to the generally recognized prescriptive rule which members of Y are supposed to follow, and which is supposed to guide the conduct of members of Y; and in (B) with reference to the practice actually prevailing among the members of Y. It will be important to keep this distinction in mind.

SUMMARY OF THE DISTINGUISHING CHARACTERISTICS OF CUSTOMS*

For any kind of act to be called a custom, it must be *regular,* at least in the temporal sense, and also (with the exception of habits and sometimes maxims) in the "general" sense of being widespread. It must also be an *act,* that is, a form of behavior which the person or persons

---

* For the reader's convenience, a schematic guide to the various forms of custom has been developed and may be found in Appendix A.

involved may either do or refrain from doing, as they choose.

Some forms of action can be subsumed under a *descriptive* rule, while others are required by *prescriptive* rule. Either type may be called *customary* under certain conditions. *Habits* are of the first type, regulations and rules of international law are of the second. Some types of "custom" admit of *both* interpretations, depending upon the context.

Consciousness and *deliberateness* are other distinguishing characteristics. Some customary acts may be done unconsciously, while others must be done with full awareness of what one is doing. A given kind of act is not a habit unless its performance is both unconscious and not deliberate. These considerations are irrelevant to other types of custom, such as style and etiquette.

For some kinds of custom, it is essential that one *believe that one ought to do* the kind of act involved; for others, it is not.

For some kinds of custom, *sanctions* may be applied for failure to conform to the customary norm; for others, they may not; and for still others, the question does not even arise.

Compulsion may be exerted by the group to secure conformity with some kinds of custom, it may not with respect to others, and with still others, the question does not arise.

Suspension may take place with some kinds of custom, but not with others, either because there is no person with authority to do so or because the question of suspension does not arise. The same is true of abolition of a customary rule.

Finally, there arises the question of the *natural law*. Some people hold that certain kinds of custom (and perhaps even *all* kinds of custom) must conform to or be derived from the natural law. This is a problem which will be discussed at length later in this study.

THE TASK AHEAD

With the completion of this analysis, and the introduction of the problems of international law and the law of nature, we have reached the outer fringe of custom. From this point on we are confronted with the manifold problems entailed in trying to define morality on the one hand, and law on the other. We must also come to grips with the relations between custom and morals, between custom and law, and between law and morals. But now that this initial study of custom has been made, now that some of the many kinds of practice that can be so denominated are familiar, and the distinctions between them and their various attributes have been pointed out, we are better prepared to undertake the task ahead.

In the section that follows, a number of theories on the relation between custom and law will be examined. These theories are fraught with difficulties and are riddled with paradoxes. I would submit that many of the difficulties are occasioned by confusion of one kind of custom with another, and that the paradoxes result from submission to the unconscious temptation to resort to persuasive definitions of crucial terms—particularly the terms "custom," "law," and "morals," or their equivalents. Part of the task in what follows, then, will be to identify those problems when they arise, to locate the source of each of them, and to try, so far as possible, to resolve them. Once this task has been completed, it may be possible to offer a theory on the nature of custom and law which will be free of such pitfalls.

Chapter II

Sources of Law

Writers on law have often referred to custom as one of the sources of law. John Chipman Gray, the American realist, says, for example, "Custom is another of the sources of law," and then he goes on to show to what extent (consistent with his theory) a judge is influenced by prevailing customs when he deliberates before rendering a decision.[1]

More recently, J. L. Brierly, referring to Article 38 of the Statutes of the International Court of Justice, which directs the Court to apply "international custom, as evidence of a general practice accepted as law," counted custom as a source of international law, but in a somewhat different sense—as evidence for the existence of law.[2] Since this subject will be discussed at some length, an inquiry will first be made into the meaning of the expression "source of law." Like "custom," "source of law" is not univocal.

Close examination reveals the variations in meaning of the word "source." Many of the arguments among philosophers of law reduce to verbal quibbles, to a failure to see

[1] J. C. Gray, *The Nature and Sources of the Law*, Second Ed. (Boston: Beacon Press, 1963, reprinted from 1921 edition published by Macmillan), 281ff.
[2] J. L. Brierly, *The Law of Nations*, Sixth Ed. (Oxford: Oxford University Press, 1963), 56, 59ff., *et passim*.

that (for example) what is a "source" for one kind of law is not a "source" for another since "source" is being used in two different senses; and that a law's having one kind of source does not preclude its having one or more other kinds as well. The following major senses of the word "source" as it applies to law may be distinguished:

CAUSES AS SOURCES OF LAW

If a historian is interested in the origin of a given law, he may seek out the conditions—social, political, historical, etc.—which "explain" that law's existence, which account for its coming to be at one time rather than at another. In general, this is the approach most historians take in their inquiries. Whether studying a particular event, such as the entry of the United States into the Second World War; a movement, such as communism or the civil rights movement; or an institution, such as the United Nations or the Red Cross—the question this kind of historian is asking is, "What is its cause; why did it come into being?" In the same way, one may inquire into the causes of laws—the events which, considered historically, explain or render intelligible their existence.

An example of historical explanations being used as "sources" of a movement or widespread attitude and state of mind is contained in the following quotation from the concluding chapter of *The Anguish of the Jews* by Father E. H. Flannery:[3]

It should be clear that the primary source of anti-Semitism stems from that which has isolated the Jew from other nations and cultures. This isolation originated in his sense of divine election, his dedication to the Law, his worship of Yahweh.

Whether the Jews' stubborn refusal to cease being Jews is the primary source of anti-Semitism is not germane to

[3] Edward H. Flannery, *The Anguish of the Jews* (New York: Macmillan, 1965), 269.

the present inquiry. But I cannot refrain from observing that Father Flannery's study makes it abundantly clear that lust, greed, avarice, lies, irrational resentments, and various kinds of individual and mass psychoses on the part of anti-Semites have played no small part as "sources" of anti-Semitism and anti-Semitic acts and events. Whether they are primary, secondary, or tertiary sources is—I suppose—a matter for historians to quibble about; but it is odd that Flannery should pass over them completely in his summary, placing the major responsibility—if we can call it that—on the Jews themselves.

At any rate, from the quotation above, and from others in the context, it seems that Flannery means the following: The Jews behave in a certain way (worshiping Yahweh, for example). This is a historical fact. This behavior, which we may call X, produces certain reactions, Y, in the minds of non-Jews. The reaction, Y, is also traceable to certain predispositions which are themselves a result of other factors, A, B, C, etc. Y, in turn, causes anti-Semitic acts, U, V, W, . . . Thus, X is the source (or, more accurately, a source) of W.

Now W might be an isolated event, such as a certain individual's shouting an epithet, painting a swastika, overturning a cemetery marker, or beating a rabbi. But it might also be an edict—prohibiting social intercourse between Jews and non-Jews, for example, or prescribing the wearing of a peaked cap or a yellow star, or revoking the licenses of Jewish physicians, or prohibiting the publication of Hebrew or Yiddish periodicals.

Thus, historical events—whether they are frequent acts by a class of persons which serve as an irritant to the ruling power, or individual acts which dramatize and bring to the surface a matter of concern—can result in, and thus be a source of, certain laws. (Single events which have had important lawmaking effects are Mordecai's refusal, according to the legend, to bow to Haman, and more recently, the assassination of President Kennedy.)

MOTIVES AS SOURCES OF LAW

We may distinguish two major senses in which motives may be regarded as sources of law: psychological and ethical.

1. Psychological Motives

In the example given immediately above, one can speak of Y as well as X as being a source of the edict W. But here we are referring not to a historical event but to a psychological motivation for the edict. Thus, among the sources of the Nuremberg Laws one might count Hitler's paranoia and the Germans' predilection for anti-Semitism. There are many psychological motives which people have for enacting various sorts of laws. Legal philosophers have listed, among others, competition, the desire to secure what one has, the desire to be esteemed by others, and fear and mistrust of outsiders.

2. Ethical Motives

In addition to their psychological motives, people have ethical motives for enacting legislation. Some laws are enacted because the people feel it is necessary to prohibit that which is evil and to encourage that which is good. Thus, the desire to achieve a just society, or a just form of government, or a fair distribution of wealth, may be regarded as a source of law.

It may not always be easy to distinguish between so-called ethical motives for laws and purely psychological ones. Hobbes said that men organized themselves into societies and set up laws because they recognized that only in this way could they fulfill their natural desire for self-preservation. Whether self-preservation is an ethical norm or not is open to question. Similarly, there are those who would argue that such motives as prudence, rational self-interest, benevolence, humanitarianism, cruelty, greed, and sadism are ultimately reducible to psychological dispositions, while others would insist that they are not. It is no concern of ours to settle this issue. It is sufficient for our purposes to indicate that one can sensibly talk about any of these as motives for, and thus as sources of, law.

LAW-ABIDING PROPENSITIES OF PEOPLE AS SOURCES OF LAW

Law can be operative only where there is a disposition on the part of the people to act in accordance with the legal norms. That such a disposition is necessary has been emphasized by many legal philosophers from John Austin to Karl Olivecrona. Austin looked upon the tendency of people to obey the commands of their sovereigns habitually, and to disobey only under the greatest provocation, as the ultimate source of law.

According to Olivecrona, a law is a command made through the machinery of the state to a populace that is psychologically conditioned to obey such commands. Here, then, two factors are necessary in addition to the command itself: (1) the disposition of the people to obey, and (2) the apparatus of the state, which consists, according to Olivecrona, of a body of persons conditioned to execute automatically the laws which are promulgated, using force where other means do not suffice. Thus, habitual obedience on the part of the people, and the existence of an effective machinery for enforcement, are two other kinds of "sources" of law—"sources" in that they are social conditions necessary for the existence and efficacy of law.

EVIDENCES OF LAW AS SOURCES OF LAW

In attempting to determine whether an alleged law, *X,* is indeed a law, a judge will seek out (or will demand that he be shown) evidence that it is. Such evidence may consist of ordinances, statutes, and judicial precedents, and in some instances of textbooks and other books by learned authors, or of journals. In the realm of international law, other evidences of law are treaties, unilateral declarations, instructions to diplomatic agents, and—most importantly for our purposes—the actual practice of the persons (i.e., the states) concerned.

It may seem odd to some that statutes, ordinances, and the like have here been classed as *evidences* or *sources* of law, for according to most ordinary usages, these are primary examples of *laws,* not of *sources* of law. It is true, of course, that they are generally thought to represent laws rather than sources of law, but there is a subtle distinction that must be made. Some legal philosophers have insisted that only what the judge decrees is law. When a layman consults his attorney, the latter will tell him what the law is; this consists, essentially, of a prediction as to what the judge will most likely decide in his case. To the legal realist, then, the law *is* what the judge decides. The statutes and ordinances passed by parliaments and congresses and other legislatures are not laws, but guides by which judges are supposed to decide cases brought before them.

If anyone would deny that the law is what the courts say it is, let him consider the role of the Supreme Court (for example) in the United States, which is as infallible in its pronouncements on what is and what is not law in the United States as the Pope is said to be in matters of faith and morals. Whether the realist is correct in his analysis of law is a question which need not detain us here. But it is certainly true that, whether we choose to regard statutes as law or not, they do serve the function described above—of guiding the judge in his decision-making process—and insofar as the judicial decision is law, the statutes, having contributed to that decision (whether as evidence of law or as premises in a legal deduction), are sources of the law.

1. Practices as Evidences of Law

A practice, it will be recalled, is a type of act which the members of a certain group regularly do, and is of such a nature that whenever one engages in that kind of action, he does so consciously and deliberately. One who acts in accordance with a practice may do so because there is a rule prescribing that he do so, or he may be acting merely as a matter of course. The term is to this extent ambiguous. In fact, it is precisely this ambiguity that raises questions in the court: First, is there a practice, as one party might allege, or not? And secondly, if there is, do those who engage in it do so "as a matter of course," or because they acknowledge the existence of obligation or duty?

It is generally held that practice counts as a ground for belief in the existence of law or as evidence of the existence of a law only where actions are performed "in the conviction of obligation," as Parry puts it.[4] Other conditions are also deemed to be necessary, at least in international law, most notably the following: (1) Concordant practice by a number of states with reference to a type of situation falling within the domain of international relations; (2) continuation or repetition of the practice over a considerable period of time; (3) conception that the practice is required by, or consistent with, prevailing international law; and (4) general acquiescence in the practice by other states.[5]

One will recognize (1) as the principle of generality —that is, regularity with respect to numbers of persons observing the practice; and (2) as the principle of regularity with respect to time. (4) is related to, but not identical with, (1); for acquiescence in a practice is not the same as participation in it. Thus, for example, one

---

[4] Cf. Clive Parry, *The Sources and Evidences of International Law* (Manchester: Manchester University Press, 1965), 63.
[5] Judge Hudson, *Yearbook of the International Law Commission*, 1950, Vol. II, 26. Cited in Parry, op. cit., 62.

state may acquiesce in other states' imposition of a twelve-mile territorial limit by not intruding into territorial waters so defined; but that state might not itself participate in the practice, for it might confine the limits of its own territorial waters to three miles, or to some other number of miles which it chooses to consider reasonable.

(3) is the condition most worthy of special note. A mere showing that a state *claims* to have a twelve-mile limit is insufficient to establish that limit as a rule of international law. The states making such claims must have "maintained them by the actual assertion of sovereignty over trespassing foreign ships. . . . The only convincing evidence of State practice is to be found in seizures, where the coastal State asserts its sovereignty over trespassing ships."[6] Here, then, the state not only *claims* that a demand-right exists on its part, and that a correlative duty exists on the part of other states, but it acts in accordance with that belief, and its actions are clear evidence that the state possesses the conviction that such rights and duties do exist. On the other hand, however, a given state's acquiescence in other states' twelve-mile limits does not constitute evidence that it accepts the limits imposed by them. Presumably it might test the claim some day by intruding within the limits which it chooses to contest, inviting seizure and either resisting the attempted seizure by force or submitting the case to adjudication.

These, then, are examples of the manner in which practices are used as evidence of international law. Insofar as such practice is in turn an evidence to which judges refer in order to determine what international law is, they are evidences (or sources, in this sense of the word) of law. In common law nations, when there is a dispute as to whether a given kind of act is permitted under the common law, evidence of the existence of a practice is regarded as evidence of the existence of a common law.

[6] *I. C. J. Reports*, 1951, 116, 191. Cited in Parry, op. cit., 63.

2. *Intentions of the Parties Concerned as Evidences of Law*

Intentions enter as a source of law when they are considered as evidence that a treaty has or has not made law. It is held by some authorities that not all treaties make law. Some treaties have the effect of being contracts between the states concerned, as, for example, trade agreements. These latter may be concluded in accordance with the contract law of one or other of the contracting states, so that no new law is thereby established. In general, these authorities say, the presumption is that international agreements do not create legal relations unless the parties expressly or impliedly declare that they are to do so. Thus, treaties become law if and only if the parties thereto intend that they shall have legal force. Hence, the intention of the parties, being necessary for the creation of a law through a treaty, is a source of law. Analogies to this may be found in municipal or domestic law. Indeed, intentions play an important role in establishing the existence of customary law as well.

AUTHORITY AS A SOURCE OF LAW

Another sense in which the phrase, "source of law," is used, is exemplified by the following: "Act *X* has as its source the power that Congress has, under the Constitution, to enact such legislation." The source of the legislation, then, is the authority by which it was enacted. One may ask, "And what is the source of *that* (i.e., the constitutional) authority?" And the usual answer is, "the will of the people," or "the consent of the states," or something to that effect. This question seems, on the surface at least, to be the same as the question which might have elicited the first comment, namely, "What is the source of Act *X*?" But I am inclined to think that we have here two different meanings of the word "source," though both of them might be reduced to "authority." (Hence, we have two different senses of "authority.")

A systematic consideration of the questions and their answers will make this clear:

(A) What is the source of Act *X?*

(B) The constitutional authority granted to Congress to enact such legislation.

(C) What is the source of the Constitution's authority (or of the Constitution)?

(D) The will of the people.

In the answer (B), that the Constitution is the source of Congress's authority to enact bills such as *X,* the word "source" is understood to mean "higher legal authority." Whenever a law is cited as justification for an act, the appeal is to a higher legal authority. The policeman justifying his arrest of a suspect, the judge sentencing a defendant, the appeals court overturning or upholding a lower court's judgment—each of these appeals to a *law* as justification for his action.

But in (D), the case is quite different. Here we are referring to the *act* (real or imagined) which serves— theoretically, at least—as the ultimate *authorization* for all *law.* To use terms borrowed from Hobbes, it is a reference, not to the law, but to the *authors* of the law, and to the act (or acts) by which they *authorized* the law.

The following analogy may be useful here. Ten years ago, the faculty of Ivy College voted on a set of bylaws which contained a provision that no member of the faculty could speak for more than two minutes on a given subject at any one meeting. Professor Smith, attending his first faculty meeting, rose to speak on an issue which he considered to be vital to the future of the college, and was silenced before he completed his introduction. Turning to Professor Jones, one of his older colleagues, he asked, "What is the source of that ruling?" And Jones replied, "Article 73 of the bylaws." "But," Smith persisted, "what is the authority for *that?*"

To which Jones replied, "A vote of the faculty which took place some years ago."

It is obvious that Jones's two replies refer to two very different things: One is a rule, the other an act on the part of a group of people which has had the effect of establishing a rule. The differences between the two are so obvious that there is no justification in dwelling upon them for too long; but I will pause just long enough to take note of one or two characteristics that are possessed by one but not the other.

The vote is (or was) an event that took place at a particular time and place. A rule is not an event at all, and though it exists in some sense, it does not occur at any particular time or place. (It may, of course, exist over a period of time.) It makes no sense to speak of suspending a vote which has already been taken and gone into effect. But a rule may be suspended. Finally, a vote cannot take place in the absence of rules governing the procedure, the majority required, eligibility of voters, etc. But rules can (and do) exist where there is no vote, as where there is rule by fiat, for example.

Thus, a rule is one sort of authority, whether it grants power to an official or an individual to perform a certain kind of act, or to establish a rule of a lower order; and a vote which authorizes the establishment of a rule—whatever the order of the rule may be—is another.

There is still another, which has been alluded to above, and that is the power of a dictator. If Castro causes a law to be enacted, someone might ask,

(E) What is the source of Act *X*?

And an appropriate reply might be,

(F) Castro's power.

Though the answer in (F) is related to those in (B) and (D), it is also different from them. When we speak of the power of a dictator as the source of the laws which he decrees, we mean something quite different from what we mean when we speak of a higher law, or the will or consent or vote of the governed as the source of law. For here we are referring more or less explicitly to the threat of sanctions which the dictator wields in order to enforce his decrees, while there is no explicit reference to sanctions in (B) or (D), and possibly no implicit reference to them either. For in spite of what some positivists have claimed, laws can exist, and have existed, in the absence of the threat, or implied threat, of sanctions.

It is easy, for example, to imagine a religious society based upon a commitment to love for all men which has rules but lacks sanctions for any of its rules. The society might have a rule requiring prayer at dawn each day, for example, but no sanctions for violation of the rule. The sect's members might be expected to adhere to the rule, not out of fear of punishment, either in this world or the next, but out of love for other members and for God. If a member, for whatever reason, should fail to follow the rule, the members might not be angry; nor would they manifest any unpleasant reactions toward him at all. They would go on loving him as before, adding (perhaps) a silent prayer for him in their daily devotions —not in such a way as to make him uncomfortable, but quietly and unobtrusively, without his knowledge. And the God to whom they would pray, being a God of love, understands his erring creatures and, far from harboring thoughts of vengeance or desires for punishment, showers his blessings upon them that their love for him might be increased and that they might thereby return to him sooner and with more devotion than before.

A doctrinaire positivist might be inclined to argue that such a "rule" is not a rule, since it has no sanctions. To this I can only reply that the argument is a clear case of *petitio principii*. The game of solitaire, after all, has rules which can be violated—for one can cheat at solitaire; but there are no sanctions for cheating at that game.

Now when we say that Castro's power is the source of the law *X*, we mean that if it were not for the power wielded by Castro, *X* would not have been enacted. Castro's power may have been both a necessary and a sufficient condition for X. And the implication would be that if Castro's power should cease to be effective, the law would cease to exist. But here, it would seem, we are referring to Castro's power as a historical precondition for the enactment of X. (This has been discussed above.) It is the power, the threat of sanctions, and the fear engendered by that threat, that explains the existence of X as a *law,* that accounts for the fact that people do, as a matter of fact, act in accordance with X and that X exerts normative force over their behavior.

Perhaps it would be desirable to disentangle several distinct but interrelated conceptions of the relationship between power and law: First, power may be a source of law in the way that civil rights demonstrations may be a source of law—as efficient causes for the enactment of the law. If Castro had not seized power in Cuba, the hotels would not have been nationalized. Secondly, there is a sense according to which he who has power wields authority and makes laws. In this sense, the dictator is a source of law just as the king, or Congress, is a source of law—that is, as legislator. And finally, we might say that since a person tends, as a matter of fact, to obey the commands of those who effectively threaten him with punishment should he disobey, we must conclude that, as a matter of observed fact, the commands of persons who wield this power tend *nolens volens* to become law. Thus, it is not so much as *lawful authority* that their commands become law, but as *potential inflicters of harm.*

Chapter III

Custom and Law

We must now concern ourselves with the question of the extent to which custom may be considered a source of law, and the sense or senses in which it may actually be a source of law. One of the most thorough analyses of custom and its relations to law is contained in Francisco Suárez's *Treatise on Laws and God the Lawgiver* (*De Legibus, ac Deo Legislatore,* 1612).[1]

Suárez begins by distinguishing *custom as fact* from *custom as law.* In most controversies as to whether there is a custom concerning a certain matter, he says, the question is in relation to custom as fact rather than custom as law.[2] He seems to have in mind here the kind of distinction which we discussed earlier, between "practices" which people perform regularly, consciously, and deliberately, and "regulations," which are sanctioned, which people believe they ought to do, which may be suspended or abolished, etc. "Custom as fact," then, would be a kind of act which people regularly perform, but which they are not obliged to perform by any moral or civil law; while "custom as law" would be a kind

[1] Published by the Carnegie Endowment for International Peace in the *Classics of International Law Series,* with translation (London: Oxford University Press, 1944).
[2] Ibid., 442.

of act which people do regularly, but which they are
also obliged to do, which they may be required to do,
and for which sanctions may be invoked against them
should they fail to do it.

He distinguishes three meanings of the word "usage"
(*usus*), from which "custom" is in some sense derived:
(1) the theological meaning, in which "usage" signifies
"an act by which the will freely carries out that which
it elects," (2) the everyday meaning, in which "usage"
signifies "a repetition of like action" or, more specifically,
"repeated, free, similar actions with respect to one
thing."[3] Finally, (3) "usage" may have the sense of
habit or *tendency,* the tendency to perform certain acts[4]
frequently as a result of constant repetition of such acts.

Suárez says that analysis of *mos* (general conduct)
and *consuetudo* (custom) reveals that their meanings
do not significantly differ from those of *usus* insofar as
attention is confined to their factual—or, as we would
say, descriptive, non-normative—characteristics. They refer to moral acts, at least in some forms of discourse.

According to Suárez, one aftereffect of frequent repetition of similar acts may be the development of a habit
or custom in the non-normative sense, but this is a purely
"factual" matter. But "a second aftereffect may be one
of the moral order, after the manner of a power or a
law binding to such action, or nullifying another obligation. This may be called consuetudinary law or a
legal rule introduced by custom."[5] Such a legal rule
establishes new powers, rights, or obligations, and thus
differs considerably from custom considered as a regular
repetition of a certain type of action.

In other words, under certain conditions, a mere practice, or habit, as these terms have been defined above,
may develop into a type of custom more closely resembling one (or perhaps more than one) of the kinds
of custom discussed in Chapter I that possess normative

[3] Ibid., 443.
[4] Ibid., 444.
[5] Ibid., 445.

or obligatory force—such as regulations, for example, or etiquette, rituals, or simple customs. In international law, it will be recalled, practices do become law, so that after a certain usage has been in effect for a length of time, rights and duties and powers devolve upon persons who did not have them before. A similar effect has taken place in civil law, but only when certain conditions are fulfilled. Let us see now under what conditions a practice may become a law, according to Suárez.

Certain conditions must be present before practices can become consuetudinary law. Among these necessary conditions is the compatibility of the original custom with natural law. It will become apparent later that to serve as sources of law, customs need not be compatible with existing positive law. A further necessary condition is that the custom have sufficent generality to be considered the "general conduct of the people," for the private conduct of a single individual, family, or small group of persons, does not have lawmaking force.[6]

Suárez's distinction between the right-making powers of individuals and the lawmaking powers of a community may not be immediately clear. Surely, one might ask, the long-established custom of an individual has right-making capacities. Consider the case of the man who has beaten a path from his home through his neighbor's land to the highway, and has used it regularly over a period of years. His continued use of the path and his neighbor's forbearance create for him a legal right of way, and for his neighbor a legal obligation to refrain from interference with his exercise of that right. Suárez would reply, however, that our path-beater has the power to create this legal right of way for himself *because of a law already in existence* which confers that power upon him; but consuetudinary law is *created* where there was no law before, and may in fact abrogate existing laws.

[6] Ibid., 447.

The private usage . . . of a single person can confer
a legal right to hold a thing, that is, ownership of a
thing [etc.]. . . . This kind of right has not the force
of law, and so it is correctly held to be not a regulative
right, since it neither prescribes nor ordains anything,
but rather a regulated right, since it has been acquired
by the operation of some law.[7]

Although private persons and "imperfect communities" may follow certain customs, these customs never
attain the status of law, according to Suárez, for a
person cannot establish a law over himself, though he
may be determined to carry out the custom which he
has set for himself. No matter how often he may repeat
a certain act, the repetition in itself is never sufficient
to establish an obligation. (An additional right-making act,
such as a promise, may establish an obligation upon a
private person to continue to act in accordance with his
custom; but the obligation arises from the promise, not
from the custom.)

One might object that in the case of a corporation or
a labor union, customary ways of doing certain things
become the proper ways to do those things and achieve
the status of law within the organization. A telephone
operator who answered customers' calls with a cheery
"Hi there!" might be deemed by the telephone company to have broken its unwritten law, established by long
and universal practice, requiring that the opening greeting be "Operator!" The company might also impose sanctions against the non-conformist, including the ultimate
sanction available to it—firing her. It would seem, then,
that within a so-called "imperfect community," customs
can achieve the force of law.

None of this, however, affects the point at issue. Suárez
undoubtedly recognized that customary rules become established within various imperfect communities. Even
within a family, long usage may establish an expectation
which may result in grave objection if it is disappointed,
and even the demand that the expectation be fulfilled. Nev-

[7] Ibid., 448.

ertheless, the family as a whole is not obligated to adhere to its custom if it (or its leader) feels that it is no longer desirable to do so. In the example given above, the operator has an obligation to the company to adhere to its customary form of greeting; but the company itself is not bound to demand that she do so. If officials of the company should decide to change the greeting from "Operator!" to "Hi there!" they would certainly have the legal right to do so, even though hundreds of millions of people may have developed a certain expectation due to long-established usage.[8]

Suárez's point may be put rather simply as follows: There are basically two kinds of communities which he chooses to recognize, "perfect" and "imperfect." An imperfect community is one which is subject to regulation from a larger community of which it is a part, while a perfect community is not—presumably either because it is not part of any larger community, being sufficient unto itself; or because even if it is a part of a larger community, it is one among equals, no authority being superior to its own. The telephone company is an imperfect community in this sense, for it is subject to regulation by the government. Thus, according to Suárez, though a practice arising within an imperfect community may become so well established as to give rise to strong expectations, it never achieves the status of customary law, since customary law properly so called exists only at the sufferance of the sovereign—that is, of the ruler of the perfect community of which the imperfect community is a part. Thus, if the sovereign learns of the existence of the telephone company's practice, he may choose either to tolerate it or to abolish it; and the "rights" and "duties" supposedly established by the custom exist in reality only if the government chooses to recognize them.

[8] Recent court decisions in which the right of the telephone company to change to the all-number dialing system in the face of fierce community opposition come to mind in this regard.

This is an unnecessarily restrictive definition of "custom." It is worthwhile to note, as Suárez does, that legal relations are ultimately dependent upon the sufferance of the larger "legal" community, so to speak; but it is a mistake to say that the customs of imperfect communities may never attain the status of law. There is a very clear sense in which they *can*. Within the imperfect community itself—the corporation, the labor union, or what have you—a practice may acquire all the attributes of a law, as has already been indicated with respect to the rebellious telephone operator, who has an obligation to answer calls in accordance with established usage, who can be disciplined if she fails to do so, and who may even be "tried" by a kind of internal court if charges are brought against her. Indeed, this "imperfect community" may even go so far as to "banish" her from its midst and to deprive her of all the rights she had previously enjoyed within the community. So long as the "custom" operates in virtually the same ways as "laws" do in the "perfect" community, there is no reason to deny that they *are* laws.

However, if one should maintain the rigid restrictions advocated by Suárez, it would be necessary to point out that certain rules which *everyone* agrees are laws would have to be excluded. For there are really very few "perfect" communities in Suárez's sense. The City of Buffalo, for example, is not a perfect community, since it cannot adopt a rule that goes contrary to the Constitution of the State of New York, or (as some say) to the public policy of the State of New York as interpreted by that State's highest court. And even the State is not a perfect community, since its laws are subject to review by the United States federal courts. It would follow, then, that a local custom which grew up in the City of Buffalo and assumed all the attributes of law is *not really* a law by Suárez's criteria. And this goes against all established usage.

Another problem which Suárez leaves unanswered is the meaning of "general conduct of the people." The terms "general" and "people" are notoriously vague, as recent attempts of the U. S. Supreme Court to define them have shown. In deciding upon what constitutes an appeal to prurient interests, for example, whose judgment shall we count? That of the most knowledgeable critics? (If so, one is faced with the additional problem of defining "knowledgeable" in this context.) Should one direct his attention to the views of the people who concern themselves most over the subject—those, for example, who support the American Civil Liberties Union on the one hand, and those who support the Legion of Decency on the other? Or should one base his judgment on the attributes expressed by the "man on the street"? If so, which man, on which street? There is some reason to believe that the "man on the street" in Coon Rapids, Iowa, is likely to have a very different outlook on many questions from his counterpart in Greenwich Village or in Cambridge, Massachusetts.[9] The opinions of men emerging from factories and construction projects may be very different from those of men emerging from the executive suites of large corporations. And what *is* the community? Is it the town in which an offense has occurred, or the state, or the entire nation? There is no need further to belabor the point. It is just as difficult to define the general opinions of the people; since it is very difficult to decide upon meaningful definitions of "general" and "people."

It is true, as stated above, that the "customs" of the imperfect community can be overruled by the laws of the perfect community of which it is a part; but this is surely not sufficient to justify our not calling them "customs" in the legal sense of the word.

[9] The most notorious example of biased sampling continues to be the Nielsen rating of television programs.

MUST CUSTOM CONFORM TO NATURAL LAW?
A REPLY TO SUÁREZ AND THE NATURAL-LAW THEORISTS

Suárez says that a custom contrary to natural law does not properly deserve to be called custom and cannot serve as a source of law, for the natural law is universally applicable and immutable. Usages contrary to natural law are more fittingly called corruptions. A custom consisting of indifferent acts[10] is outside the natural law, and, unless it possesses some useful characteristics, can have no influence on the making of law. A custom which is in accordance with the law of nature does not have law-making capacities, since the law already exists. However, it may serve to "strengthen" the natural law by promoting its observance among men. More importantly, it may serve to interpret the law of nature.

Suárez's views on natural law follow closely the traditional doctrines as they are expounded in St. Thomas Aquinas and elsewhere. Cutting through the mass of verbiage on this subject is no easy matter, for wherever one turns in the literature of law and political theory, one finds discussions of the natural law, each author offering his own interpretation of the "law of nature" and of its relations to positive law. I shall argue that this view of the dependence of custom upon the natural law is in-

---

[10] An indifferent act is one which is neither good nor bad. St. Thomas Aquinas denied that any human act is indifferent in this sense, but the Scotists maintained that such acts as picking a straw from the ground are indifferent. Another example might be the order in which one puts on one's socks, or whether one puts on both shoes and then ties the laces, or ties the lace of the first shoe before putting on the second. Suárez has followed the Scotist opinion.

Incidentally, even such seemingly trivial questions as those I have raised in this note are treated in the Code of Jewish Law. There, specific regulations are laid down for just such matters as which shoe ought to be put on first. Cf. *Kitzur Shulchan Aruch*, opening chapters.

correct on the grounds that (1) there is no natural law, and (2) even if there were natural law, there would be other more satisfactory ways of solving the problems the natural-law theory is supposed to solve. In its essentials, the natural-law theory can be reduced to one or both of the following claims: (1) There is a law which is observed by all peoples, and is common to the whole human race. This law is a direct result of human nature (or of the nature of society, or of divine regulation of the universe), universal, eternal, and immutable. (2) There is a law, based upon human nature (or the nature of society, or God's creative will) which serves as a standard by which all human laws are to be judged. Any so-called human law which is not consistent with (or, according to some authorities, *derived from*) this natural law is in reality no law at all, and consequently exerts no binding force upon the persons to whom it is directed.

The first claim, presented here in as pure a form as I can distill (this version incorporates direct quotations from Justinian's *Institutes*), has been purged, as far as possible, of the normative terms which invariably creep into natural-law theorists' discussions, in order to provide as good a contrast and as clear a distinction as possible between the two interpretations, (1) and (2). (1) is an empirical claim, to the effect that certain laws may be found wherever one turns; that there are certain laws which will be found to be in effect in every human society, without exception. What these laws are is specified differently by each author. It is therefore difficult to decide whether the empirical claim is true. If the claim is taken as a strictly empirical claim, it seems to be false. Even the author of the *Institutes,* in the very paragraph in which he said that the natural law was "observed amongst all people alike," felt constrained to note that slavery, which is contrary to the natural law, is practiced by some people. The same unhappy admission must be made, it seems, about every other rule which the natural-law theorists have brought forth as an example of a universally observed law. Indeed, natural-law defenders of slavery are not lacking. It would not be difficult to multiply examples, but it is not necessary to do so here.

It may be objected that when the natural-law theorist speaks of the natural law being "observed" universally, he does not mean that everyone acts in accordance with the law; he means at most that ideally, everyone will act in accordance with it, since human nature is such that society's interests can best be served if people do act in accordance with the natural law; or that all rational men act in accordance with the natural law, or recognize that people ought to do so; or that only pathological societies[11] or governments disregard the natural law. But each of these alternatives brings in the very normative elements that we had attempted to purge from this definition, and reduces it to a variation of (2), which will be considered next. Thus, such terms as "ideally," "best," "rational," "ought," and "pathological" are all normative, or evaluative. They introduce an element which renders the proposition such that it cannot be verified by any purely empirical means—such that it is no longer purely descriptive.

If attention is directed to the second alternative, or to those normative revisions of the first, one finds that there are new problems, which are every bit as difficult to resolve as those which confront the first.

First, there is an epistemological problem. How can we ever know what the natural law is and what it requires? Natural-law theorists themselves have reached no consensus here. They have thus far been unable to devise a decision procedure by means of which the skeptic might discover for himself what is and what is not in accordance with the natural law. When they tell us that any rational man knows—or can easily discover for himself—what the dictates of the natural law are, it sounds very much as though they are begging the question, using "rational" in such a way that only those who do make the expected discoveries are deemed to be rational. One cannot help remarking that—difficult as it is to say this, in the light of the events which have transpired during the last half cen-

---

[11] Cf. Lucas, op. cit., 327ff. *et passim.*

tury—the word "pathological" seems also to be question-begging in this context.

Secondly, the second version of the natural-law theory raises theoretical problems in the philosophy of law.

First, consider the view that all laws must be derived from the natural law. As before, one is confronted with the problem of finding out what the natural law requires. But even if there were a complete listing of the laws of nature, it is not at all clear how all the laws of a constantly evolving society could possibly be derived from them. Presumably, there is a finite, and probably (according to most authorities) a very small number of principles of the natural law. Assuming that they include a procedure for deducing principles, as the geometrician does from his elements, there would still be a potentially large, but ultimately closed, finite system of derivative laws. It is very difficult to conceive of such laws being sufficiently adaptable to be applicable to both a feudal monarchy, for example, and a modern democracy. Difficult, that is, unless the principles of the natural law are themselves so vacuous as to allow of a broad variety of interpretations. But if this is the case, then, of course, it is difficult to see what possible use they might have.

Similar objections might be urged against the view that positive law, to be law at all, must be consistent with the natural law. And, in addition, it may be asked, what does it mean to say that the "so-called" positive law is no law unless it is consistent with the natural law? Does it follow that the man on the street is not obliged to obey such a putative law? Even if it has been duly passed by the legislature, and is enforced by the courts and the executive? It would seem, on the surface, to have all the marks of law. To whom is he to turn for guidance in so important a matter? Whether there is an external authority or not is irrelevant. The ultimate authority, according to the natural-law theorist, is conscience (possibly the rational, healthy conscience), since what we are dealing with is a form of moral decision. I may be obliged to obey the law in the sense that I am obliged to hand over my money to the man who holds a gun to my head, but I am not *morally* obliged to obey it if it is wicked, pathological, or insane. So says the defender of the natural law.

Recent experience with the Nazis demands of us that we find some way to justify what seems to us the eminently reasonable (but difficult) proposition that those who collaborated with Hitler and willingly complied with his vicious and unjust laws have behaved criminally and ought to be punished. In fact, it is always in a context of this sort that questions of natural law arise: For the natural law is invoked by the Establishment to justify a law which is being challenged, by the critics of an existing law as a justification for civil disobedience or rebellion, or by those who would punish "criminals" who have acted under color of law. But one need not insist that the unjust law is no law in order to justify disobedience. One may admit that it is law, but insist that since it is unjust, it shall not be obeyed.

With respect to the problem of punishing those who have acted iniquitously under color of law, one can, as Hart has suggested, invoke frankly retrospective legislation. Such legislation may, in general, be undesirable; but it may be the least of the three evils (i.e., denying that legislation which had been on the books, and was enforced by the ruling power, was law; letting a vicious, monstrous act go unpunished; or invoking retrospective legislation). As Hart puts it, if we invoke the first of these alternatives—that which would be advocated by the natural-law theorists—"we confuse one of the most powerful, because it is the simplest, forms of moral criticism. If with the Utilitarians we speak plainly, we say that laws may be law but too evil to be obeyed."[12] Surely no one

[12] Cf. H. L. A. Hart, "Positivism and the Separation of Law and Morals," *Harvard Law Review* (1958), reprinted in Olafson, *Society, Law, and Morality* (Englewood Cliffs, New Jersey: Prentice-Hall, 1961), 462ff., where he discusses the case of a German woman who, in order to rid herself of her unwanted husband, reported his anti-Nazi statements to the

would suggest that *ex post facto* laws be widely employed, or be employed on a regular basis. The danger inherent in such a policy is evident to all. But Hart, and others, would maintain that the danger of invoking such legislation when there is evidence of governmental sanction of iniquitous behavior in order to punish those who have engaged in such behavior is less than that which is inherent in confusing the issue of what is and what is not legal. That is legal which is in conformity with the law, and law is what has been adopted by the state in accordance with certain procedures and forms, and is enforced by whatever judicial and other enforcing agencies the state may have; and the iniquity of a law makes it no less a law. If we follow the views of the natural-law theorist, we must conclude that there can be no bad law, no iniquitous law—and this leads to confusion when a rule seems, on every other ground, to be a law like any other. What we must cultivate, according to Hart, is the ability to discriminate between laws which are and laws which are not iniquitous, and, I would add, the courage to work for the overthrow of those that are and, if necessary, to suffer the consequences of violating them.

Those who argue against Hart's view of retrospective legislation contend that the evil inherent in adopting this view is that no man can know, with any degree of certainty, whether his act, performed today and under today's laws, will not someday be judged under some other laws.[13] But neither can he know, with any degree of certainty, whether he will not someday be judged by the standard of some "natural" law whose contents have never been made known to him, which he is admittedly incapable of

authorities, who then tried him and sentenced him to death. For a different point of view, and a different account of the case in point, see L. Fuller, "Positivism and Fidelity to Law: A Reply to Professor Hart," from the same volume of *HLR,* also reprinted in Olafson, 488ff. For Hart's later views, cf. *The Concept of Law* (Oxford: Oxford University Press, 1961), 354f.

[13] J. R. Lucas, *The Principles of Politics* (Oxford: Oxford University Press, 1966), 228f., 340f.

knowing (if he is "irrational" or "iniquitous"), and which directly conflicts with the laws which seem to him—on every show of evidence—to be the legitimate laws of the state in which he resides.

We thus find ourselves impaled upon the horns of a dilemma, if we want to punish those who have acted iniquitously under color of law: Either we expand the meaning of "law" to include the natural law, or we invoke retrospective legislation. Whether we adopt the first or the second of these alternatives, there is no way for a person whose fate is to be decided to know in advance that his act, which seemed to him at the time to be lawful, would later be deemed unlawful. If we adopt the first alternative, we must invoke principles which are admitted, even by their defenders, to be vague, and we must resort to such question-begging assertions as the following: "If ever people knew that they were doing wrong, the Nazi leaders must have known." But we do save two important legal-moral principles: *Nullum crimen sine lege,* and *Nulla poena sine lege;* for, by extending the term "lex" to include the so-called natural law, we have a law condemning as criminal the acts we choose to condemn, and prescribing penalties for them. If, on the other hand, we adopt the second alternative, we may be as clear and precise as we please, and we may save ourselves from one kind of question-begging by engaging in another: passing *ad hoc* legislation to fit the crimes and penalties to the acts we choose to punish. Here, too, we may "save" the two principles mentioned above by extending the word "lex" to apply to the new, retroactive legislation. Neither horn of the dilemma is particularly attractive.

There is, of course, an alternative, which impales us upon a new dilemma: not punishing the alleged criminal at all. Now either we have the right to punish a criminal or we do not. If we do, we are faced with the first dilemma. And if we agree that we do not, we are in effect granting unlimited license to the ruling power, acquiescing in the despot's claim to unlimited sovereignty, to his assertion, *"L'état, c'est moi."*

These problems arise because our institutions work adequately only in the generality of cases. There is a decision procedure for virtually every problem that comes before the courts in the normal flow of human events; and under normal circumstances, men are not faced with the moral question, whether to obey or disobey the law. It is taken for granted that they will obey, and when they disobey, few people will question the propriety of their being punished. This is, as I have said, in *normal* circumstances. But unfortunately, some cases are *not* normal. They are so abnormal that no institutions have been developed to accommodate them. The courts have had no procedures handed down to them for handling the exceptionally hard cases, nor have they developed such procedures themselves, since they have seldom, if ever, been confronted with such cases before. And as for the people, it matters not whether one invokes a higher, "natural" law as a justification for their rebelling against a system they regard as iniquitous—claiming that the laws which they are disobeying are no laws at all and that there is consequently nothing illegal about their disobedience—or a moral rule to the effect that though the law is law, and though legal penalties may be exacted by the authorities against those who disobey, the law is evil and ought to be overthrown. The end result is the same. When conditions become sufficiently bad, the people revolt. They leave it to the philosophers to rationalize for them after the fact. And similarly, when circumstances are so abnormal as to be virtually without precedent, they will find ways to accommodate themselves and their institutions and the procedures of those institutions to the new circumstances. When their spirit cries out for punishment of those who have offended their standards of decency to such a degree that they will not let normal standards of legal practice stand in the way of their demand, the offenders will be punished, and the philosophers and the lawyers will be left to worry later over the rationale behind their actions, and their theoretical implications.

In the last analysis, these "standards of decency" may well be determined by *mores* peculiar to a particular society, or to a particular segment of a society, and not by the absolute, universally applicable standards in which the natural-law theorists would have one believe.

It must be concluded, then, that the natural law is not a useful way of dealing with the highly unusual, even abnormal situations which are usually claimed by natural-law theorists to be insoluble without an appeal to the natural law, nor need it be invoked to justify unusual actions taken in such situations. Any such justification is bound to be fraught with difficulties, for the institutions and procedures concerned are not equipped to deal with the highly unusual case, and other justifications can as easily be found. Entirely new theoretical constructs may be required. Thus far, though, none has emerged able to withstand the tests of criticism.[14]

---

[14] This kind of situation is not unique to the moral and legal sciences. We find analogous problems in the physical sciences. The well-known problem of the nature of light, for example, bears remarkable resemblances to our problem. Certain phenomena convinced early investigators into the nature of light that light must be composed of particles. Later, however, other phenomena were discovered which could in no way be subsumed under the particle theory, but were easily explainable under the assumption that light was a form of wave. Since waves are propagated only through media, this led to the hypothesis that space is filled with a nebulously defined medium called the "ether." Further investigations revealed that neither the wave theory nor the particle theory would accommodate all of the observed phenomena. This led to the introduction of entirely new concepts, and to the abandonment of the "ether" hypothesis. New, unusual, and unexpected phenomena had to be explained. The first attempts consisted of efforts to fit them into the old conceptual frameworks. When that failed, new concepts were evolved. Philosophers of law are still trying to squeeze certain facts into molds which simply don't fit. Whether it is because human affairs are matters of great delicacy, or because legal philosophers are men of conservative bent or small imagination, the fact remains that the physicists have attacked their problem boldly and imaginatively, and in the past seventy-five years have made tremendous progress in their efforts to make sense of the phenomena they investigate; while

These, then, are some of the reasons for rejecting the natural-law approach of Suárez and others, but they are not the only ones. Some of the other reasons which lead us to reject the natural-law theory have been around for a very long time indeed.

One cannot help but wonder why legal theorists continue to stumble over the confusions which David Hume so masterfully disentangled over two hundred years ago. "Nothing can be more unphilosophical," he said, "than those systems, which assert, that virtue is the same with what is natural, and vice with what is unnatural."[15] For, as he went on to explain, "natural" has a number of senses, depending upon the context:

(1) A natural event may be compared to one that is miraculous. Miracles, of course, are unnatural occurrences. But even the most incurable optimist would hesitate to affirm that it takes divine intervention to bring about human iniquity.

(2) We sometimes call what is rare or unusual "unnatural," while what is common is called "natural." But vice is unhappily all too common to be called "unnatural" in this sense—and some cynics contend that virtue is so rare as to be utterly unnatural.

(3) "Natural" is sometimes contrasted with "artificial." Under this interpretation, natural-law protagonists, in admonishing us to follow nature and to look upon what is unnatural as evil, would be urging us to spurn the artificial and the synthetic. This is reminiscent of Pope Paul's ban on artificial forms of birth control on the ground that they are not "natural." Such reasoning, if carried to its logical conclusion, would lead to the rejection of every form of manufactured object: the homes in which we dwell, the conveyances in which we ride, the utensils with which we cook, the knives and forks with which we eat, and the very clothes with which we cover our natural

---

in the past thousand years, virtually nothing new has been introduced into the natural-law controversy.

[15] David Hume, *A Treatise of Human Nature,* Book III, Part I, Sec. 2, Selby-Biggs (ed.), 475.

nakedness—to say nothing of such "unnatural" means of alleviating human misery as novocain, the sulfa drugs, tranquilizers, and aspirin.

To Hume's list, John Stuart Mill added the conception of regularity[16]—the kind of regularity which constitutes the laws of physics, chemistry, and the other natural sciences. The law of gravity is an excellent example of such a regularity or natural law.

It makes no sense to urge people to obey the law of gravity, for by no force of will are they capable of *disobeying* it! Surely obedience to the law of gravity is no virtue. If it were, every falling stone would be behaving virtuously. Since it is impossible to disobey the law of gravity, or any other law of nature (in this sense), evil, vice, and iniquity would under this definition of "nature" be impossible. For according to the natural-law theorist, vice is defined as acting contrary to the laws of nature. If the laws of nature are identified as those regularities which take place invariably in the observed world, then one cannot act contrary to them. Hence, under this view, no act may properly be defined as evil. This, of course, is rather remote from anything any natural-law theorist would want to say.

Before dismissing the natural-law theory, the theory of St. Thomas Aquinas should be considered. According to Aquinas,

> Each thing is inclined naturally to an operation that is suitable to its form: thus fire is inclined to give heat. Wherefore, since the rational soul is the proper form of man, there is in every man a natural inclination to act according to reason: and this is to act according to virtue. Consequently, considered thus, all acts of virtue are prescribed by the natural law: since each one's reason naturally dictates to him to act virtuously.[17]

16 J. S. Mill, *Nature,* available in a number of editions.
17 *Summa Theologica,* a. 94, Art. 3. Tr. by Fathers of the English Dominican Province (London: Burns, Oates & Washburne, 1912–25).

Without entering into a lengthy review of Aristotelian and Thomistic metaphysics, some elucidation of this passage may be helpful.

Everything, he states, has certain natural tendencies or dispositions. Thus, fire naturally tends to warm things, water naturally tends to make them wet, acorns tend to grow into oak trees, and so on. Man's most distinctive natural characteristic is his rationality. He possesses, therefore, a natural tendency to act in accordance with reason. Now it so happens that the dictates of reason are identical with virtue. Virtue is never unreasonable. Thus, since man naturally tends to be rational, and since rational acts are also virtuous, it follows that man naturally tends to act virtuously. Since reason operates in accordance with nature—or, more correctly, in accordance with the natural law—it follows that virtue is acting in accordance with the natural law.

It is a little difficult to accept this. After all, if man were naturally inclined to be rational—and hence virtuous—how could we account for the very large number of vicious men? How could we account for the many cases of murder, theft, adultery, and assault, to say nothing of the many unkind acts of which we are all guilty? It would seem that many of us, or possibly most of us, are failing to act in accordance with our natural inclinations.

It seems very odd to say that we are naturally inclined to behave in a certain way, and to say in the same breath that we very often don't act that way at all. If fire often failed to give heat, we would have legitimate grounds for doubting whether it had a natural tendency to do so. If acorns frequently sprouted into rosebushes or grapevines, we would be less apt to assert that they had a natural disposition to grow into oak trees. In the same way, in view of the significant proportion of irrational, vicious acts committed by men, we have sufficient reason to wonder about the truth of Aquinas's thesis.

In fact, it seems more reasonable to say that man naturally tends to behave *destructively* and *irrationally* and in ways which are just the opposite of most definitions of virtue. According to this view, it is only the artificial restraints imposed upon men by society, or by those in authority, which constrain them to behave at all decently. Take away these artificial restraints, as William Golding did in *Lord of the Flies,* and man would seem quickly to revert to the most primitive forms of savagery.

It seems, then, that Aquinas's thesis is either so obscure and vague as to be virtually meaningless (what, after all, does he *mean* by "natural inclination"?), or else it is simply false. In all fairness, we must not suppose that he makes no attempt to deal with these problems. He does, but his efforts are completely unsuccessful. For example, he says that

> the natural law, according to general principles, is the same for all, both as to rectitude and as to knowledge. But as to certain matters of detail, which are conclusions, as it were, of those general principles, it is the same for all in the majority of cases; . . . and yet in some few cases it may fail, both as to rectitude, by reason of certain obstacles (just as natures subject to generation and corruption fail in some few cases on account of some obstacle), and as to knowledge, since in some the reason is perverted by passion, or evil habit, or an evil disposition of nature; thus, formerly, theft, although it is expressly contrary to the natural law, was not considered wrong among the Germans, as Julius Caesar relates.[18]

This passage may be explained in the following way: The acorn has a natural inclination to grow into a large, spreading oak tree. But under certain circumstances, this natural inclination may be thwarted. Thus, as a result of disease, lack of water, insufficient sunshine, sterile soil, or the digestive juices of a squirrel, it may never be able to fulfill its destiny. Similarly, a man's moral growth may be impeded by disease, improper education, evil companions, an inhospitable environment, or an excessively passionate disposition to such a degree that instead of becoming

[18] Ibid., Q. 94, Art. 5.

rational, and thus morally virtuous, he becomes irrational and corrupt. And just as an entire mountainside may become sterile and barren after it has been swept by a forest fire or a disease, so also may whole societies become corrupt, as did ancient Germany in Aquinas's example—or, for that matter, modern Germany.

Although there are many weaknesses in this explanation, I shall confine my discussion to two of them. First, when we are not clear what a "natural inclination" is, it is rather difficult to speak of *the* natural inclination of any particular thing or class of things. The very suggestion that acorns, fires, or men have *one* natural inclination or one "proper" natural inclination is plainly false—at least in any ordinary sense of the words. Thus, an acorn has many dispositions, depending upon our point of view and the circumstances. When it falls into a certain kind of soil, under certain conditions of moisture, temperature, and sunlight, it has a disposition to grow into an oak tree. But under other conditions, it has a disposition to rot, under others it tends to dry up, and under still others (when it is ingested by a squirrel), it has a disposition to become squirrel meat, hair, bone, blood, and excreta. To choose *one* of these as *the* natural disposition of the acorn is arbitrary and question-begging. Fire has a disposition to give off heat, but it also has dispositions to blind, to maim, to kill, to hurt, to cook, to sear, to transform, to be beneficial, and to destroy. Under certain circumstances, it has the interesting disposition to go out.

Similarly, man has dispositions to eat and to drink, to laugh and play, and to cry and grieve; to seek warmth and comfort, and to acquire and defend material things; to give vent to his sexual impulses and to repress them; to love and to hate; to pray and to desecrate; to envy, to steal, and to kill; to give aid to the sick and weary, and to inflict bestial tortures upon men of alien cultures or heretical beliefs. Which of these are natural and which unnatural? Unless "natural" and "unnatural" are given some emotive connotation—the former one of approval and the latter one of disapproval—any of these inclinations is as natural as any other. Though we may call such sexual deviations as lesbianism and exhibitionism "unnatural," we mean by this nothing more than that most people do not behave in this way, and that we do not approve of such behavior. But in other important senses, these forms of behavior are perfectly natural.

Secondly, though the natural-law theorist masquerades behind a façade of scientific objectivity, he is neither scientific nor objective. His judgments are not the inevitable product of pure reason—whatever that is—but of the social norms of his culture. One can imagine an Eskimo natural-law theorist writing a treatise in which he would declare: "Infanticide and patricide are expressly permitted under the natural law, and as a form of the hospitality due to strangers, the natural law specifically requires that a man should offer his wife to them during the duration of their visits. Also, in order to avoid the unnecessary spilling of blood, the natural law requires that men shall settle their disputes by engaging in singing contests. Reports from the barbarous lands to the south indicate that the primitive natives who inhabit the temperate zones share a strange, backward culture known as Christianity. Instead of mercifully allowing starving, crippled, or deformed children and sick and senile elders to pass peacefully to the world beyond the stars, they enforce a mean and dreary and miserable existence upon them. Unmindful of the virtues of hospitality and generosity, they have artificially introduced a crime which they call *adultery*, forbidding the sharing of women. They have done this in spite of the insuperable difficulties of preventing men and women from following their natural inclinations, which are manifestly generous in this area. Worst of all, they settle their disputes, not like rational, civilized people, by engaging in song contests, but by destroying one another in accordance with fiendish techniques and contrivances invented by their most ingenious followers." So might a primitive natural-law philosopher write about some of our ways.

These, then, are some of the reasons for rejecting the

natural-law approach of Suárez and others. It should now be apparent that there is no need to adopt the view that custom must be in conformity with the natural law. If a custom should arise which is so grotesque, in someone's opinion, as to require extirpation, it will not further the argument to refuse to call it a custom, on the flimsy ground that it is not consistent with some principle which is alleged to be part of the natural law. If the purported custom fills all the rest of the conditions which other customs of a given type fulfill, then it would seem perverse for one to refuse to call it a custom. The only possible reason one might have for such refusal is discussed in the next section.

LAW AND CUSTOM AS PRESCRIPTIONS: DOES EITHER HAVE PRIORITY OVER THE OTHER?

Like "law" and its relatives, "custom" serves not only a descriptive function; it has a prescriptive function as well. "Law" and "custom" are both "pro" words in some contexts. (It will be seen that, in other contexts, they may be "con" words.) Thus, for example, when one is urging a reluctant friend to drive within the speed limits, one might say, "But George, it's the law!" Besides all its descriptive and predictive connotations (you might lose your license, you might be fined, the legislature passed a measure prohibiting driving over such-and-such a speed on this road, etc.), there is a certain sense of approval or disapproval, praise or blame, attached to the word uttered in such a context. Among other things, George's friend's utterance says to George, "What you are doing is bad, I disapprove of your conduct, society disapproves, down with such recklessness!" And, if it is not already implicit in some of these formulations, we might add for the sake of completeness that the utterance carries with it a certain hortatory or imperative force, "You ought to reduce your speed, stop driving so fast!"

"Custom" is like "law" in this respect. Thus, when the

native Mississippian says to his guest from New York, who has been calling the colored maid "Mrs. Johnson," "Around here, it's customary for white folks to call colored folks by their first names," his statement has certain descriptive content, corresponding to the characteristics of the relevant kind of custom set forth above in Chapter I. That people regularly do it, that it has been so for a long time, that certain kinds of sanctions are invoked against those who don't do it, and so on. But in addition, when the native makes this kind of statement to the stranger, his statement may have the same connotations of approval or disapproval, or praise or blame, as its counterpart using "law." Thus, in saying, "Around *here* the custom is to call colored folks by their first names," the native may be implying, "What you're doing is bad, I disapprove of your conduct, society disapproves, down with such abominably poor taste!" And, like the "law" statement discussed above, it has its hortatory or imperative implications: "You ought to do as we do! Call her 'Mary,' not 'Mrs. Johnson'!"

In both of these examples, "law" and "custom" have been applied to practices of which the speaker approved and which he commended to his auditor. But in certain other contexts, just the opposite is true. This is particularly evident when law is contrasted with custom, or when either law or custom is contrasted with morals.

When law and custom are contrasted with one another, in most instances one is being praised or commended, while the other is merely being described. There is no formal criterion, however, for telling which is being commended and which is being described.

Thus, for example, if peyote had been outlawed, the following conversation might have taken place between a Hobbesian philosopher and a member of the Native American Church:

PHILOSOPHER: Peyote chewing may be a custom among your people, but it's contrary to law!

INDIAN: Peyote chewing may be contrary to law, but it's a custom among my people!

The philosopher, recognizing that these Indians have a long-standing custom of chewing peyote, but believing that the law ought to be observed whether it conflicts with custom or not, urges his listener to give up peyote chewing since it conflicts with the law. But the Indian, recognizing that the law prohibits peyote chewing, insists that since peyote chewing is a custom of his people, it should be continued—whether it conflicts with the law or not.

If one should object to this example on the ground that it represents a conflict of cultures, and is therefore a special case, I would reply that other examples abound in which that kind of conflict does not exist. A very similar conversation might have taken place during Prohibition. The American people were not alcoholics, after all. But the law conflicted with a deeply-ingrained set of social customs. And as a wedding toast was being offered, someone might have objected, "But that's against the law," to which an appropriate response would have been, "Of course it's against the law, but it's our custom." Notice that the two speakers are in agreement on the facts of the case. Each of them acknowledges that drinking a toast at weddings is customary, and each acknowledges that it is illegal. Their differences are differences in attitude. The objector sets a higher value (in this instance) on adherence to law than he does on adherence to custom, while in this particular instance, the reverse is the case with the other speaker. The first speaker uses "custom" descriptively, without normative force, while the second speaker uses "law" in the same way. But the first speaker commends adherence to law in this case, while the second commends adherence to custom, each of them adding—as it were—a certain normative emphasis to the word as he utters it, or (perhaps) taking advantage of the commendatory, "pro" connotations that the words he emphasizes have.

Notice that I stressed that each speaker took the stand he took relative to custom and law *in this instance*. This is so because most of us are seldom (if ever) confronted with such a choice; and when we are, there is no guarantee that our priorities will be consistent. If a man has committed himself to a Hobbesian philosophy of law, according to which he is always obliged to follow the commands of the sovereign, he will probably be pretty consistent in his judgments on conflicts between custom and law. But ordinary men do not make such commitments. They are inclined, instead, to judge each case as it comes along and to act according to their interests as they see them at that time. If no great harm is likely to be forthcoming from violation of the law, they are likely to prefer continued observance of the custom. If the custom is deeply ingrained, they may take grave risks in order to perpetuate what is—to them—very precious, even though it is condemned by the majesty of the law. And this may be so even where the custom at issue—like the consumption of alcoholic beverages—is not connected with religious rites and is not believed to be a moral duty.

LAW AND MORALS AS PRESCRIPTIONS: THE PRIORITY OF MORALS TO LAW

Turning now to the other kind of contrast—that between morals on the one hand and law or custom on the other—one finds that the situation is quite different. In *most,* but not *all* instances in which such a comparison is made, it is to the detriment of law or custom. The hortatory emphasis is placed upon the moral duty. Whenever a real conflict arises, a very high value is placed upon the duty to conform to the law or the custom—so high, indeed, that it becomes tantamount to being a moral duty itself. Thus, philosophers are wont to extol the virtues of obedience to the law in terms that leave no doubt that breaking the law is tantamount to breach, not only of a legal obligation, but of a moral obligation as well. Who can ever forget Socrates' impassioned defense, in the *Crito,* of the view that a violation of the laws of the

state is also a violation of the highest moral norms; that
certain *moral obligations,* comparable to those which one
owes to one's parents, are owing to the state; and that
even if the law works to one's greatest disadvantage (requiring one's execution), one has nevertheless a moral—
not just a legal—duty not to thwart its operation.

High as the duty to obey the law may be, where there
is a conflict between one's moral duty and one's legal duty,
most people seem to feel that moral duty takes precedence. Indeed, according to some philosophers, moral
prescriptions are "distinctively characterized" by the fact
that they either "demand precedence over any conflicting
lines of conduct," or—in the case of the least stringent
kinds of moral obligations—may be preferred over other
kinds of obligation, which may justifiably be overlooked
or neglected in order to carry out the moral obligation.[19]

Thus, the following conversation, typical of so many
that are heard on college campuses today, may be instructive:

JONES: You ought to refuse to be inducted into the Army.
SMITH: But my draft board called me.
JONES: Nevertheless, you should refuse.
SMITH: Surely I ought not to refuse. The law stipulates
    that every person who is called by his draft board
    must report for induction.
JONES: I know that you have a *legal* obligation to submit
    to induction. But that's all it is—just a *legal* obligation.
    You have a *moral* obligation *not* to submit to in-
    duction; and therefore, you ought to refuse to be
    inducted.

The priority of the moral norm to the legal norm is
clearly assumed by Jones. If the conversation were to
continue, Smith would not be likely to dispute that. The
argument would revolve, not around the question of the

[19] John Ladd, *Structure of a Moral Code* (Cambridge, Massachusetts: Harvard University Press, 1957), 104.

priority of moral to legal norms, but about whether Smith does or does not have a moral duty to refuse to submit to induction.

CUSTOM AND MORALS:
THE PRIORITY OF MORALS TO CUSTOM

The very same result emerges when we find people discussing alleged conflicts between customary norms and moral norms. If the dispute were, for example, about the custom of toasting a newly married couple, and Smith contended that it was required by social custom while Jones insisted that it was an immoral practice, the dialogue would *not* be likely to proceed along the following lines.

JONES: I know very well that toasting newlyweds is required by social custom, but it is forbidden by moral law, and you ought therefore to refrain from the practice yourself, and urge others to do the same.

SMITH: The first part of what you say is true. I know as well as you do that it's immoral to toast newlyweds. And we agree also that it's required by social custom. It's priorities that we disagree about, because custom takes precedence over morals. Therefore I ought not only to follow the practice myself, but to encourage others to do so as well.

This dialogue, I say, is not likely to take place, because under one interpretation, Smith's comments make no sense, and under the only other one that is at all plausible, it introduces considerations which we rule out by hypothesis for reasons that will soon become apparent. Some special advantage accruing to Smith from defying the rules of morality and acting in accordance with custom is ruled out as well. (The man who cheats on his income tax might provide a contemporary smalltime example of this. Or the man who observes the social customs of the South, though he knows that they are immoral, because by doing so he ensures himself of financial success, while by doing otherwise he would hurt his business.) The intrusion of this special advantage clouds the issue; for it introduces a special motive for Smith's choice, different from either custom or morals considered alone.

As a second alternative, it might be assumed that Smith is simply informing Jones about the facts of life— that as a matter of fact, people regularly flout their moral obligations and do instead what they are accustomed to doing. But he goes further than this, adding a value judgment of his own—that he *ought* to do likewise. This, then, is not a plausible interpretation.

The only interpretation remaining is that Smith must be talking nonsense. For if we assume that Jones and Smith are two men of ordinary manners and morals, and that neither of them has anything special to gain from following one course of action rather than the other, then we must conclude that when Smith claims that custom takes precedence over morals, he is revealing his ignorance of the meaning of "morals"; for as we have said above, moral obligations are prior to all others by *definition*—or so it would seem, if we can judge from the way people use these terms in actual ethical disagreements. The usual course of a dialogue such as the one recounted above would require Smith, if he disagrees with Jones as to the propriety of drinking toasts to newlyweds, to challenge Jones's assertion that drinking toasts is immoral.

I conclude, then, that there is no necessary order of priority between law and custom, one taking precedence in certain contexts, and the other in others. But whenever a given practice is required either by custom or by law, but forbidden by moral considerations, the moral rule takes precedence.

EXCEPTIONS TO THE RULE OF MORAL PRIORITY

The only class of possible exceptions to the primacy of morality over law and custom which I can conceive of would be those positive rules of morality (the "Thou shalts," as opposed to the prohibitions, "Thou shalt nots") which might be prohibited by social custom or by law. Thus, for example, I may have a positive duty to marry several wives in order to "be fruitful and multiply and fill up the earth," as the Bible commands. But the law prohibits my doing so. It seems to me that most people would agree that here the legal prohibiton must take precedence over the moral injunction. There is no apparent absurdity in saying here that the legal obligation has priority over the moral.

Suppose—to take another example—that I firmly believe that I have a moral obligation to tithe my earnings for charity, but that the government taxes my earnings at such a high rate that I cannot possibly contribute a tenth of my income to charity. Few people would be inclined to declare such a law to be iniquitous or to demand that it be disobeyed for the sake of the tithe, or to demand that any government which prevents its citizens from contributing a tenth of their incomes to charity be overthrown. It's hard to imagine anyone, except perhaps an Old Testament prophet, making such an absolute out of the injunction to tithe one's income.

In general, positive moral duties (which may be called *moral injunctions*) are usually deemed to be less absolutely binding than negative moral duties (which may be called *moral prohibitions*). Except for those moral injunctions which are really only disguised moral prohibitions (such as, "Whenever you speak, you must tell the truth," which is equivalent to "You must never lie"), most moral injunctions give a wide latitude of choice as to the time, the manner, and the frequency of performance. Thus, the injunction to give charity leaves the agent a wide range of choices as to the charities he may choose to support, the frequency with which he makes contributions to them, and the amount he gives to each or to all. (The injunction to tithe obviously sets a lower limit on the amount, but the other options are left open, except in certain cases, where a portion of the tithe is to be set aside for the priesthood, for example.) In this respect, they differ radically from moral prohibitions. For if *at any time whatever* one fails to do what the prohibition commands (that is, if one does what the prohibition forbids), one has *ipso facto* failed to observe the prohibition. However, if *at any time* one fails to do what the injunction commands, one has not *ipso facto* failed to observe the injunction, for it is always possible to fulfill it at some future date, or to have fulfilled it at some past time. In other words, if there is ever a single instant in which I commit murder, I have thereby violated the prohibition against murder. But there may be many occasions on which I do not give charity; but I am not thereby violating the injunction, so long as I give charity *sometimes*. As Ladd has put it, "if we exclude those injunctions which are prohibitions in disguise, we must conclude that injunctions cannot be reduced to prohibitions of non-performances."[20]

Ladd has also made a useful distinction between moral *counsels* and moral *injunctions*. Moral *injunctions* are those positive precepts which are *obligatory,* having a high degree of "stringency," while moral *counsels* are considered to be *right,* and their performance *praiseworthy;* and they are of a lesser degree of stringency. The former are compared to the "precepts" of Christian moralists and to Kant's "perfect duties," and the latter to "counsels of perfection" and "imperfect duties."

Moral counsels are usually considered to be *right,* that is, falling somewhere between being obligatory and being indifferent. One can perhaps describe them best by saying that one has a duty to act in accordance with moral counsels, and the more he does, the more he is to be esteemed as a moral man. One who failed to observe *any* of the moral counsels would not be deemed a villain (assuming that he never violated any moral prohibitions), but he would not be called a good man, either. One who observed some moral counsels would be called a good man; and one who was especially zealous about observing them would be called saintly.

[20] Ladd, op. cit., 122.

The sum of this, so far as we are concerned, is the following: In order to fulfill one's duty with regard to moral counsels, it is sufficient to perform them sometimes and under some circumstances, and it is not necessary to perform them at all times and under all circumstances. Further, it may be sufficient to fulfill only some of them. If, for some reason, one cannot fulfill all of them, one is not thereby deemed to be a wicked person or to have committed a moral crime.

For this reason, perhaps, we can see why positive moral duties are not usually deemed to have priority over legal or even customary prohibitions. The point is that *prohibitions, whatever* their status—customary, legal, or moral —are usually looked upon as having prior claim, or superior authority, over affirmative duties. Failure to abide by prohibitions is usually followed by more stringent sanctions than is failure to act in accordance with positive injunctions. Where there is a conflict between a prohibition and an injunction, in most cases the prohibition will be deemed to have priority. Of course, there are degrees of stringency among prohibitions as among injunctions, and a strong injunction will take precedence over a weak prohibition. (For example, few people will doubt that the injunction to save a drowning boy's life will take precedence over the "No Swimming" ordinance.) But as a general rule, most prohibitions take priority over most injunctions, particularly those injunctions which are counsels rather than disguised prohibitions. Although this qualification may vitiate, to some extent, the general principle that moral rules have priority—virtually by definition— over other kinds of rules, it seems nevertheless to be the case. But this concession does no real harm to the general principle. For the principal moral injunction at issue here is the general one, that one ought to do as much as possible to act in accordance with the moral counsels and to fulfill as many of them as one can as often as one can. This is a very loose kind of rule, permitting of many degrees of fulfillment and many variations in the method of fulfillment. Thus, if a specific moral injunction falls into conflict with a legal or customary prohibition, there is no serious threat to one who wants to do his moral duty. He may still do his duty—his general duty, that is—even though he may not be able to fulfill this particular injunction. There are, after all, plenty of other moral injunctions which he can observe. And if some avenues to sainthood are cut off by law or custom, the prospective saint may throw himself all the more zealously into the fulfillment of those injunctions which are permitted him by custom and law.

A serious conflict would arise, then, only where one is living in a society which is so iniquitous that virtually *all* moral injunctions are forbidden by social pressure (whether that pressure is exerted through formal means—through the law—or informally—through customary prohibitions).

Although religion should not be equated with morals, since there are certain important differences, a useful analogy may be drawn from the experiences of the Jews in the Soviet Union. If a Jewish housewife is forbidden to kindle her Sabbath candles by a fire ordinance, she and her family will miss this traditional observance. They may long for it, and they will regret having to forgo the ceremony; but they will feel that the law must take precedence, and they will find some other ways in which to express their religious fervor. The religious injunction, then, does *not* take priority over the legal prohibition. If the state prohibits the baking of matzah, rendering it impossible to fulfill the command that matzah be eaten on the Passover, the Jews will feel a sense of deprivation, but they will find ways to compensate for the loss. If social custom is such that men are expected *not* to cover their heads in public places, the religious Jew—to avoid embarrassment and possible ostracism—will uncover his head, feeling that this, after all, is but one of many ways in which he can demonstrate his fear of God. But if *every* outward manifestation of religious devotion is forbidden, if *every* channel is closed, if the state through its laws and the people through the exertion of informal pressures render it impossible for the Jew to practice *any* of the positive commandments of his religion—then the general religious injunction, that one ought to fulfill as many of the positive commands as one can as often as one can, is itself being thwarted; and here the spirit rebels. For the Jews can rightly claim that their religion is being destroyed—a claim which they could not have made if only a few of their practices were forbidden. And here, I think, the religious man would say that the religious law must take precedence over the legal and social prohibitions that had interfered with its observance.

In a similar fashion, if only a few moral injunctions are frustrated, and if one can find others which may be fulfilled, one feels no compulsion to defy the law or the expectations of one's associates. But where the pressures extend over a wide spectrum of activities, prohibiting all or most of the things one deems to be morally desirable, then one feels constrained to insist that the laws are bad, that the customs of the place are evil, and that the time has come to replace them with others that do not interfere with one's spiritual or moral growth.

SUMMARY OF CONCLUSIONS REACHED IN THIS CHAPTER

This discussion may be summarized by relating it to Suárez's views:

Suárez is wrong in asserting that a given practice must conform to the natural law before it can be called "custom," for there are insuperable obstacles to our acceptance of the notion of natural law, and there is no good reason to refuse to call a custom that is immoral a bad *custom*.

Suárez is wrong in asserting that "imperfect communities" cannot establish customs of their own. First of all, the term "imperfect community" seems to include communities which obviously do establish laws and customs. And secondly, in many senses in which the term "custom" is ordinarily used, it makes perfectly good sense to say that imperfect communities establish their own customs, and we find in fact that they do.

Suárez's assumption that imperfect communities cannot establish custom was partially based upon his further assumption that custom is ultimately dependent upon the consent of the sovereign. This assumption will be examined shortly. But it should be apparent from the foregoing that if this means that law always takes precedence where there is a conflict between custom and law, it simply does not square with the way people behave. On the contrary, there seems to be no linguistic difficulty in saying that custom should, in some cases, be prior to law. Such a statement would indicate that nothing in the concept of "law" militates against the view that law need not (logically) always take precedence. On the contrary, on those frequent occasions when people prefer a custom to a law with which it conflicts, this is due neither to failure to understand the meanings of the terms nor to moral perversity. If, however, Suárez is saying that law *ought* always to take precedence, then it would seem that he owes us some defense of this view. No doubt a case can be made for it, but thus far, no one, to my knowledge, has made such a case.

Suárez's discussion of the natural law should not be confused with a demand (or a recommendation) that custom be subordinate to morals, or that when there is a conflict between moral duties and consuetudinary duties, the former should prevail. However, in taking up this problem, it was observed that whenever people find that there is such a conflict, they invariably agree that the moral duty takes precedence when the moral duty is a *prohibition* of an act *enjoined* by custom. When the reverse obtains, however, there are fewer compunctions about complying with the customary prescription, so long as compliance with other moral counsels is permitted.

In addition, it was noted that like "law," "custom" has, in addition to its descriptive meanings, a certain normative, commendatory, hortatory, or prescriptive force. In certain contexts, it is used not only to describe the way in which people actually do behave, or to predict the likely consequences of a given course of action (e.g., that certain sanctions will be invoked), but also to urge the auditor to follow the course of action being described, to commend it to him, and to indicate approval of those who do follow it and disapproval of those who do not.

Chapter IV

Law Conceived as a Kind of Custom

CUSTOM AND THE LAW OF NATIONS

In this chapter I shall discuss custom and its relations to international law. The positivists refuse to acknowledge the very existence of international law, because (as they say) the word "law" cannot appropriately be applied to the relations between sovereign states. I shall argue that this demonstrates, not that there is no law of nations, but rather that the positivist conception of law is basically inadequate to deal with such laws.

In the last chapter I rejected the natural-law theory, to which appeal has frequently been made for a justification for and understanding of the law of nations. If the natural law is rejected, and if (as I shall argue) the various positivist conceptions of law cannot provide a basis for international law, then it is necessary to find some other conception of law that will. I propose to show that *custom conceived as constitutive of law* provides that basis. I shall begin, then, by discussing the positivist conception of the relations between custom and law.

THE POSITIVIST CONCEPTION OF THE
RELATIONS OF CUSTOM TO LAW

Some positivist philosophers (such as Hobbes, Spinoza, John Austin, Pufendorf, and others) have denied that there is any positive international law. If this is so, it would follow, of course, that there is no customary international law.

As anyone who is familiar with Hobbes's political philosophy would expect, Hobbes completely denies the capacity of custom to effect changes in *any* positive law or to give rise to any kind of legal obligation. Since the sovereign alone has the capacity to make or abrogate law, his consent, either express or tacit, is a *sine qua non* for any law. Without his consent, no law can be made and none can be abrogated. Hence, it would follow that if the people should establish a custom which happens to be contrary to the will of the sovereign, and even if that custom should be observed for a very long time while the sovereign was unaware of its existence, it would have no legal effect whatsoever. The sovereign would be under no obligation to permit its continued observance once he learned of it, and might specifically condemn and prohibit it if he so desired. Furthermore, any person who observed such a custom, knowing that it was contrary to law, would to that extent be breaking his covenant with every other citizen, no matter how widespread such observance had been prior to his act. Finally, it would also follow from the fact that the sovereign's consent is a necessary condition for the establishment of law that where there is no sovereign, as between nations, custom can never have any lawmaking effect whatsoever, or—to use my former terminology—custom may never serve as a source of law.

In *De Cive*, Hobbes distinguishes between two kinds of civil law: written and unwritten. Any law which has been promulgated, in whatever form (in writing or orally) is a written law:

> By written, I understand that which wants a voice, or some other sign of the will of the legislator, that it may become a law. For all kinds of law are of the same age with mankind, both in nature and time, and therefore of more antiquity than the invention of let-

ters, and the art of writing. Wherefore not a writing, but a voice is necessary for a written law; this alone is requisite to the being, that to the remembrance of a law. For we read, that laws, contracted into metre, were wont to be sung.[1]

The unwritten law, however, is not customary law but "that which wants no other publishing than the voice of nature or natural reasons; such are the laws of nature."[2] Customs, even those established by judicial interpretations of the laws, are not laws unless they have the sovereign's consent. "They are to be received among the written laws, not for the custom's sake (which by its own force doth not constitute a law) but for the will of the supreme commander. . . ."[3]

Again, in *Leviathan* he says, "When long use obtains the authority of a law, it is not the length of time that makes the authority but the will of the sovereign signified by his silence, for silence is sometimes an argument of consent; and it is no longer law than the sovereign shall be silent therein."[4] Suppose, however, that a land has been conquered, but that the people continue to observe their ancient usages. Surely then law does not flow from the sovereign, who had nothing to do with the establishment of those usages? Even in such a case, says Hobbes, such usages "are the civil laws of the victor and not of the vanquished commonwealth. For the legislator is he, not by whose authority the laws were first made, but by whose authority they now continue to be laws."[5]

Thus, if the various provinces of a given commonwealth observe widely divergent usages, "we are not to understand that such customs have their force only from length of time, but that they were anciently laws written

[1] Thomas Hobbes, *De Cive*, Sterling P. Lamprecht (ed.) (New York: Appleton-Century-Crofts, 1949), Chapter xiv, Sec. 14. 164.
[2] Ibid.
[3] *De Cive*, Chapter xiv, Sec. 15, 165.
[4] *Leviathan*, Part II, Chapter xxvi.
[5] Ibid.

or otherwise made known for the constitutions and statutes of their sovereigns, and are now laws, not by virtue of the prescription of time, but by the constitutions of their present sovereigns."[6]

Law is by its very nature a command, and as such it can exist only where there is someone who has the authority to give commands. Hobbes carefully distinguishes between law and counsel, and also between law and covenant. "Law is the command of that person . . . whose precept contains in it the reason of obedience; that is, . . . the precepts . . . of all the powerful in respect of them who cannot resist, may be termed their laws."[7] One therefore obeys a law because of the power of the one who commands, but one obeys a counsel because he deems it desirable to do so. Thus, counsel is given to and obeyed by those who are willing, while even the unwilling are subject to the dictates of the laws. "The right of the law-giver is not abrogated at the pleasure of him who hath a law imposed."[8] Hobbes takes Aristotle to task for having defined "law" in such a way as to make it equivalent to "contract" or "common consent."[9] According to Hobbes, if Aristotle really believes that laws are "nothing else but naked and weak contracts," then he has confounded two very different things, for contracts have no obligatory force (except in conscience) before a sovereign power has been instituted, and may, under such conditions (i.e., in the state of nature) be carried out or left unfulfilled at pleasure. The difference is that while a law is a command, a contract is merely a promise; a man is under a moral obligation to fulfill his contracts, but the law compels him to obey through fear of punishment that will follow his failure to do so. Civil laws are "nothing else but the commands of him who hath the chief authority in the city, for direction of the future actions of his citizens."[10]

[6] Ibid.
[7] *De Cive,* Chapter xiv, Sec. 1, 155.
[8] Ibid., 156.
[9] *De Cive,* Chapter xiv, Sec. 1, 156f. and note.
[10] Ibid., and Chapter vi, Sec. 9, 74f.

IMPLICATIONS OF POSITIVISM FOR
INTERNATIONAL LAW AND FOR PRIMITIVE LAW

Since the nations of the world are in a state of nature relative to one another, according to Hobbes, having established no sovereign power having both the authority to promulgate laws that would bind them and the power to enforce such laws, it follows that there is no international law in Hobbes's system,[11] and therefore *a fortiori* that there is no customary law of nations.[12]

Primitive societies lack the hierarchy of courts with their judges, lawyers, and prosecutors, the army of sheriffs, jailers, and parole officers and police officers whose duty it is to enforce the laws, and the great libraries of tomes in which the laws may be found, either in the ordinances of the legislatures or in the decisions of judges. And, what is perhaps most important, they lack any formal body which is empowered to make law or to judge cases. From a positivist point of view, then, there can be no primitive law, either.

Hobbes's political philosophy is admirable for its precision of language and thought and for the elegant way in which its parts are developed and made to depend one upon the other. But his assumption that the sovereign must directly and consciously sanction all law reveals an exceedingly narrow conception of the nature and origins of law.

CRITIQUE OF THE POSITIVIST POSITION

In spite of Hobbes's ringing dictum that "during the time men live without a common power to keep them in

---

[11] Cf., e.g., Otto Gierke, *Natural Law and the Theory of Society: 1500 to 1800,* tr. by Sir Ernest Barker (Boston: Beacon Press, 1957), 289, note 63.

[12] See Appendix B for a discussion of other philosophers of law who have held similar views.

awe, they are in that condition which is called war, and such a war as is of every man against every man,"[13] it is not strictly correct to say that primitive peoples live in anarchy. The early theories which held that primitive peoples had no conception of crime, of liability, of private property, and of the distinction between accident and design have not been borne out by anthropological investigations. If one is tempted to assume, along with some of the older thinkers in this field, that primitive man is the slave of custom and that there is no law in his dealings with his neighbors, he would do well to weigh carefully William Seagle's conclusion: "The court of the bush," he says, "is nonetheless a court because it does not sit every day, because it may not always employ compulsory process, because it is not housed in a permanent structure upon whose lintel is inscribed *Fiat justitia ruat caelum.*"[14] If the existence of rights and duties is a test for the existence of law, then there is ample evidence that primitive men have law. Their law may be primitive by comparison with that of the modern state. It may be less flexible. But to deny that it is *law* is again to construe the meaning of *law* so narrowly that it can apply only to institutions which are directly comparable to our own formal legal institutions. The court of the bush and the International Court of Justice are legal institutions— primitive in some respects, but invested with the power to make judicial decisions and determinations, to render verdicts affecting the interests, the rights, the duties, the powers, and the liabilities of the people who come under their jurisdiction. Primitive men are governed by law, though their institutions have not developed as fully or as formally as have ours.

The case for international law is very much the same. Here too, the institutions are weak and often ineffective; but there exist circumstances in which the institutions set up to govern nations (so far as it is possible for them to be

[13] *Leviathan*, Part I, Chapter xiii.
[14] *The History of Law*, first published as *The Quest for Law* in 1941 (New York: Tudor Press, 1954), 34.

governed, at this stage of the law's development) function notably well. The law of nations possesses at least one enormous advantage over primitive law: It has been codified, written about, and commented upon at great length by wise and reputable scholars and jurists. Shall we say that these scholars and jurists have codified laws which are no laws, and are writing learned articles and books about figments of the imagination, shams, delusions? Scholars have been known to do such things in the past, of course. All the learned works on Ptolemaic epicycles, on phlogiston, and on the ether have long since been relegated to the back shelves of libraries where other noble but misguided efforts are stored. Will a positivistic conception of law someday come to prevail, much as the Copernican astronomy has prevailed over Ptolemaic astronomy? So that someday, students of the law will look back with amusement upon the antiquated and mistaken idea that there could be a law of nations where there is no sovereign to legislate and to enforce the laws—much as astronomers today look back upon the Ptolemaic epicycles, as physicists look upon the phlogiston and ether theories, and as biologists look upon the theory of spontaneous generation —at one time all respected theories, but now thoroughly discredited? Is it at all likely that this will come to pass?

From the fact that learned scholars study the law of nations, it does not follow that there is a law of nations for them to study. But there is one form of evidence for the existence of international law which is virtually decisive: namely, international practice. The nations of the world *behave as if there were a law governing their actions.* Each nation claims that it obeys the law, and that its adversaries have violated it. From time to time, a nation will acknowledge that it has violated the law, and will make such amends as it can. The rather nebulous "community" of nations sometimes acts in concert to apply sanctions against those who are judged to have violated the law and to enforce coercive measures against those who are reluctant to obey the law. But these, though the most dramatic, are the least instructive evidences for the existence of international law. Their very newsworthiness is some indication of their rarity. It is their rarity that shows how general is the *conformity* to international law: how seldom the terms of commercial transactions involving great sums of money are broken when states are parties to the transactions; how seldom agreements and treaties are broken; how generally vessels of all nations ply the seas without molesting one another, adhering to the rules that govern all, respecting the rights of one another; how universally diplomatic courtesies are extended and respected, and how seldom they are violated; and similarly for other kinds of cases. When people behave as if there were some law governing their actions, there is strong reason to believe that in some sense, at least, there *is* such a law.

The chief objection to Hobbes's (and the other positivists') theory is that it excludes from the definition of "law" many kinds of rules which *are* laws, such as customary laws, primitive law, and international law.

No doubt this appears to be begging the question. The positivist might reply that it will hardly do to object to a definition of law which precludes the possibility of there being international law or to maintain that the definition's preclusion of international law is evidence of its weakness. But the fact remains that such an objection is really a very strong one. If there is a body of "law" which bears many of the characteristics of other rules that are admittedly laws, that people are accustomed to call "law," and that can usefully be described as "law," and if a philosopher comes along with a definition which is so restrictive that this body of "law" is excluded from its scope, there is good ground for rejecting the definition. First, because it does not square with actual usage; for the usage, both of the general public and of the experts in the field, whether they be sociologists, anthropologists, or legal scholars, admits the designations of primitive, international, and customary law. And if it be objected that a philosopher has the right to introduce a stipulative definition, a technical definition as it were, of a term for whatever theoretical purposes he may have, I reply, secondly, that he ought to be fully aware of the fact that that is what he is doing, and he ought to advise his readers as well that that is what he is doing. If he fails to do so, it can rightly be suspected, either that he was not aware that he was departing from ordinary usage, or that he knew that he was but was offering a *persuasive definition*—urging others, in this case, to adopt this new restriction of the usage of "law" for the sake of certain theoretical considerations.

Now, Hobbes's theory is very elegant, and it would do it violence to insist that his definition of "law" is too restrictive. If, for the sake of the theory, it is necessary to adopt Hobbes's technical terminology, let us by all means do so; but we ought not, at the same time, to suppose that we are thereby watching a *demonstration* of the alleged fact that the sovereign's command is both necessary and sufficient for the existence of law. Rather, this is part of what we granted when we admitted Hobbes's definition of "law." Or if, on the other hand, we suppose that Hobbes has been trying to urge upon us a new restriction of the term "law," we have every right to reject his suggestion on the ground that far from clarifying matters, it would only confuse them. For such a restrictive definition flies in the face of ordinary (both lay and professional) usage, and if widely adopted, would make it difficult for people to communicate about matters that are of the greatest importance. On pragmatic grounds, then, we have a perfect right to turn down the invitation. If it were accepted, there would still remain a body of rules—more or less closely resembling those rules which Hobbes is unwilling to denominate "laws"—for which a new title would have to be invented, owing to the fact that we would still want to talk about them. And furthermore, there are grave difficulties in the Hobbesian theory itself, which make it very doubtful whether the theory can be applied at all. Without going into detail, it should be sufficient to note that if the sanction of a sovereign is necessary for the existence of a law, then there must be no laws in the United States of America; for in spite of all the best efforts put forth by the positivists from Austin to this day,[15] no one has yet been able to locate the sovereign of the United States.

It may be replied that in a broader form, the positivist view can be successfully defended. If we assume that every law is a command, not of a sovereign necessarily, but of the authority—whoever that may be—in the state which issues ordinances and originates laws, then we may have a definition that is as applicable to the United States as it would be to the most absolute monarchy. The commands, we might say, are issued, for the federal government at least, by Congress, usually in concert with the President, whose signature (in most cases) converts a bill into law.

But what shall we say of the case, which arises every day in one court or another, which the judge is called upon to decide but for which no clear legislation has ever been passed? The judge renders a verdict, basing his decision in part upon an exegesis of the law into which he may very well read rights or duties which were never intended by the legislators who wrote and passed the original bill. With the rapid progress of science and technology, it is impossible that the laws passed by Congress and by various other legislatures should anticipate every contingency. Thus, whether we will it or no, the courts decide cases, not only—and perhaps even not largely—upon the original true intentions of the framers of the laws, whatever they may have been, but by adjusting and adapting them to fit current conditions and needs. Hermann Kantorowicz called such rules, derived from legal exegesis, "dogmas," which he defined as "rules which are recognized as binding, not because they are commands of a personal authority . . . but because they are logically implied by other rules the validity of which

---

[15] See John Austin's awkward contortions as he attempts to squeeze the United States Constitution into his formula in Lecture VI of *The Province of Jurisprudence Determined* (London: Weidenfeld and Nicholson, 1954), 248ff.

has already been recognized." But the kind of "logical implication" to which he is here referring is interesting. It is not related to any kind of traditional or syllogistic reasoning. It is, rather, a process of "unending mutual adaptation, completion and elimination," in which we do not base the validity of one rule upon the other, but rather "adapt rule *B* to rule *A,* and conversely, with the result that they become *A*(1) and *B*(1) and so on *ad infinitum.*"[16]

Though Kantorowicz's terminology is somewhat misleading, this is nevertheless an accurate account of the nature of judicial review. Whether the procedure should be dignified with the title "logic" is not germane to the present inquiry, though so long as it is made clear that the term is not being used in its usual technical sense (which is generally confined to deductive and inductive reasoning), there is no reason why we should refuse to call this kind of judicial reasoning "logic."

The point is that the "command" theory of law is far too narrow to give an adequate account of the law. It is based upon a conception of "law" that does not do justice to the way in which the law actually operates, or to the vast complexity of legal systems and the richness of the term "law" as it is used in genuine legal discourse.

"Law" refers, for example, to the procedures of the courts. Lawyers, judges, witnesses, and jurors, as well as other persons involved in the judicial process, must behave in accordance with certain forms. These forms, however, have not been laid down by a legislature; nor have they been decreed or promulgated by a sovereign. Whatever their origin (the historical facts are not pertinent to our inquiry), it surely makes no sense today to say that they are the commands of the sovereign, or of the legislature.

"Law" also refers to the Constitution's provisions— whether they be those of the Constitution of the United

16 H. Kantorowicz, *The Definition of Law* (Cambridge: Cambridge University Press, 1958), 31.

States, which have been reduced to writing, or those of the Constitution of Great Britain, which have not. There is no meaningful sense in which the laws of the Constitution—whether of the United States or of Great Britain—can be reduced to any kind of command. The United States Constitution may more readily be compared to a covenant (though there are certain problems even with that comparison) in which the parties agree with one another to abide by certain rules.

The mistake lies in concentrating exclusively on one aspect of law, or upon law looked at from one point of view. When one looks at law from the point of view of the legislator, it appears to be what the legislator decrees it to be; and when one looks at it from the point of view of the lawyer concerned about winning cases or the judge who must make a decision in a hard case, law seems to be what the judge deems it to be; and finally, from the point of view of a citizen deciding whether to follow a given course of action or not, the law may (in certain circumstances) be what the police enforce, with some (but not necessarily much) reliance upon what the legislature and the courts have done.

THE UNWRITTEN LAW AND HORIZONTAL SOCIETIES

By setting aside these relatively narrow points of view, and attempting to determine what is common to all of them, it may be possible to find the root meaning of "law" and thus to formulate a definition that will not only solve the problems raised by legal positivism, but also dissolve the paradoxes of legal realism and other legal theories as well.

Whether we consider law from the point of view of the legislator, the judge, the policeman, or the citizen, it is obvious that its fundamental purpose is to regulate— that is, to make regular—human behavior. It is no accident that so many puzzles have been generated by the term "law" as a result of its many uses, both descriptive and prescriptive. For in its original signification, "law" could properly have been applied to any regular series of events, whether those events simply occurred in a regular fashion as a matter of objective fact (as do the phases of the moon, sunrise and sunset, and the falling of heavy objects), or as a result of prescriptive acts, such as those involved in the promulgation of a rule.

It might be instructive to follow the example of the philosophers of the Middle Ages and the Renaissance by considering the etymology of some of these terms, together with certain well-known facts of linguistic transformation.

Some sounds and phonemes, and their corresponding letters in written languages, tend to interchange with certain others—usually those belonging to the same family. Thus, dental sounds tend to interchange with other dental sounds, labials with other labials, gutturals with gutturals, and so on. In fact, the 'b' in "labial" is a good example of this phenomenon, interchanging with the "p" of "lip." The same thing has happened with "triple" and "treble," "sever" and "separate," and the word "kidnap," which was originally *kid-nab*. Instead of saying "I have to go," most people tend to say "I hafta go." Similarly, the liquids "l" and "r" frequently interchange, as evidenced by the tendency of Chinese to pronounce r's like l's, and of Japanese to pronounce l's like r's.[17]

It's easy to see how one gets "legislate" from *lex*. But one seldom considers applying the same principle to "regulate." Everyone knows that "regulate" and "regular" are derived from the Latin *regula;* but few people would connect *regula* with *rex*, the Latin word for "king." And fewer still would notice the connection between *rex* and *lex*. A king is one who regulates his subjects, who brings order into their lives; and whether one calls this activity "regulation" from *rex* or "legislation" from *lex* is a matter of indifference.

[17] Compare the following examples from Hebrew: *nashal,* to slip off=*nashar,* to fall out of; *ḥevel,* rope=*ḥavar,* to join together; *shalshelet=sharsheret,* chain; *gal'in=gar'in,* seed.

But regulation need not always be willful activity. Some things *are* regular simply as a matter of fact. One's expectations are seldom disappointed where nature is concerned: Spring always comes at about the same time, the sap runs, the buds swell, the birds return from the south, the insects begin to hum, and humankind becomes in general more passionate. In nature there is regularity without regulation and—in spite of what some theologians would have people believe—no evidence of a regulator or a *rex*. In human affairs, too, there is much regularity that is not attributable to willful or deliberate regulation or legislation. Even in supposedly advanced societies, behavior is governed more by custom than by law in the usual sense of that word. One seldom has occasion to consider the laws of the state, for relatively few of one's ordinary activities are governed by them, and few people are ever called upon by the legal organs of the state to answer for their actions.

Instead, the need for uniformity is filled by various kinds of custom: by rules of etiquette, by rituals, by styles and fashions and usages, by habits and practices of all sorts. When traveling in a foreign country with an alien culture, one is seldom troubled by ignorance of the laws of the land; the traveler's greatest source of distress is his ignorance of the ways of the people, of their customs, of the rules that govern their daily lives.

A well-known anthropologist is reputed to have suggested to someone who commented on the alleged slavery of primitive man to custom that he observe an American or British family at dinner. No rules are more rigidly enforced, no sanctions more regularly applied, than those attached to the eating habits of Western man. But there are other rules—some of which have been compiled and codified by such experts as Emily Post, Amy Vanderbilt, and Eleanor Roosevelt, though many others have not—governing modes of speech, modes of address, the manner in which one ought to walk, sit, and stand in a great variety of circumstances, courting, mourning, rejoicing, and so on. Even the distance that ought to be maintained between two persons as they converse with one another is governed by an unwritten rule that is well known, but not usually articulated, by everyone in a given culture. Persons from some countries tend to put their faces much closer together than do North Americans during informal conversations; thus the discomfort many North Americans feel when talking to them.

An anthropologist from another planet observing our behavior would certainly be entitled to conclude that it is regular and that it is governed by law—by law in the original sense, not in the Austinian sense. For he might come from a society which has many laws in this sense, but none in the Austinian sense.

Observing Western society, he might discover that it is a rather complex conglomerate of various kinds of subsocieties, each governing certain aspects of the lives of its members, with some overlapping from one to the other.

Studying the political system, he might observe that it possesses what could be called a vertical structure: a hierarchy of officials empowered to issue orders of various sorts to lower levels and receive them from the higher levels. He would note that examples of this vertical system are to be found in the courts of the United States federal government and in those of the individual states. The legislatures of the states he would find to be similarly hierarchical. He would discover that the supreme law of the land is the United States Constitution; that Congress must pass no law that violates a provision of the Constitution; that no state legislature may pass a law that contravenes a law passed by Congress; and that no county or local legislature may pass a law that is inconsistent with state law. The lower levels he would discover to be governed by the higher levels, and the ordinary citizen governed by them all, so long as he is within their jurisdiction.

But, supposing that the visiting anthropologist were familiar with a different, less hierarchical, system on his own planet, he might carry his investigation to other parts of the earth to discover whether its inhabitants had developed horizontal as well as vertical societies. It would not be long before he would find that many societies run along lines more familiar to him. He would find people whose lives were quite orderly, whose expectations were fulfilled at least as often as those of people in Western societies, who possessed rights and duties relative to one another, who had a strong sense of right and wrong, of virtue and vice, of what is permitted and what is forbidden, and who generally (but not always) acted in accordance with their norms. In one important respect, however, these societies would differ from the typical Western society: They would possess no legislative or judicial hierarchy, nothing even remotely resembling a sovereign. No one in them would issue commands or orders or promulgate laws; there would be no single agency empowered to enforce the norms of the society. Just the same the people in them would behave as if they were governed by law.

Like human beings everywhere and under any system, the members of such societies would occasionally violate their norms. If the violation were serious enough, the consequences would be completely predictable and would therefore be lawlike. In one such society, for instance, a victim and his family might retaliate with force against the violator and his family. (Law, remember, merely guarantees regularity; it does not necessarily guarantee non-violence. On the contrary, law governs violence and may on some occasions require it.) Relying on self-help and on fraternal bonds, the two families would settle their dispute in accordance with the usages of their society, for law is pre-eminently a regular and rule-governed means of settling disputes. Our visitor, being from another planet, would recognize that the feud was simply one more rule-governed means of settling a dispute. He would note its similarities to trials he had observed in Western societies, where the adversary technique has been developed to such perfection. Having studied history books, he would recall some of the older methods of dealing with disputes—trial by ordeal and trial by battle—and would correctly conclude that the family feud was but one among many techniques developed by human beings for settling their disputes in an orderly, rule-governed, though not necessarily peaceful way.

Being from a peace-loving planet, he might deplore this particular technique, but he would not for that reason refuse to call it legal; being the regular practice in that society, it would be the law of that society—a bad law, but still a law. Being from a planet that loves truth and compromise, he would deplore the adversary procedure employed in the courts of the United States, since that procedure many times conceals from the jury facts that might be pertinent to the case, and severely limits the options open to it. And it would be extremely difficult for him to understand why the jury should be permitted to render only guilty or innocent verdicts to one or more specific charges instead of being permitted to render a compromise verdict after weighing and considering *all* the relevant facts. But since this is the regular practice in the United States, he would unhesitatingly concede that it is law, though in his judgment it would have to be regarded as bad law.

The people of these non-Western societies under study by our extraterrestrial visitor go about their business in a perfectly orderly fashion: They trade, make love, raise families, educate their young, initiate adolescents, bury the dead, mend the wounded and heal the sick, pray and worship and break taboos, quarrel and threaten and fight with one another, make and break agreements—but most often keep them—and settle their disagreements by violent feuds that are carried on in accordance with time-honored traditions. No one in these societies ever issues an order to the general population, for no one has either the power or the authority to do so; and no one ever goes to anyone else for mediation of a dispute, since that is not an acceptable method for settling disagreements.

The visitor finds the basic structure of these societies so similar to his own, in that they too completely lack a hierarchical structure, that he calls them horizontal socie-

ties. He doesn't suppose for one moment that they are not
governed by law, for he has never read Austin or Hobbes
and is thus not confined to a narrow, culture-bound concept of law that automatically rules many non-Western societies—both literally and figuratively—out of court.

On reading the newspapers, he discovers that this planet,
in fact, possesses the greatest horizontal society of all.
It quickly becomes apparent to him that the behavior of
the nations of this world is governed by law, insofar as
their mutual relations are concerned. Like the individuals
in the primitive societies he has studied, they trade with
one another; they conclude agreements which they usually
keep and occasionally break; they bury the dead, mend
the wounded and heal the sick, and even establish world-
wide organizations to carry on those functions; they engage in a great variety of rituals and sometimes break
taboos; they quarrel and threaten and fight with one another, and sometimes settle their disagreements by violent
feuds which are carried on in accordance with time-
honored traditions. No one ever issues an order to the
general community of nations, for no one has either the
power or the authority to do so. The visitor discovers
that these nations have developed a variety of methods
for settling disputes—including mediation, arbitration, and
adjudication before a body of wise men known as the
World Court. But he finds that their ultimate apppeal is
always to self-help, and every member of the community
jealously guards its right to fall back on self-help whenever it feels compelled to do so.

Again, the visitor has no trouble recognizing that law
is at work here. He is not at all disturbed by his inability to find a sovereign, for he does not consider the
existence of a sovereign to be a necessary condition for
the existence of law.

There are horizontal societies, then, as well as vertical
ones, and the former are governed by law as much as
the latter. Even within the most highly developed vertical societies, some aspects of life are governed by laws
more closely resembling those of a horizontal society

than those by which the state governs them. For the sake of convenience, some philosophers have distinguished such unwritten laws from the "official" laws of the state by calling the former "customs." There is no harm in doing this, so long as one does not suppose that the customs have less force or validity than the "official" laws, or that they are effective only so long as the "official" lawmakers consent to permit them to remain operative. The truth is rather the reverse: Official laws remain operative only to the extent that they do not contravene long-established customs, as the peyote-chewing Indian and the cocktail-consuming American (discussed above) illustrate.

Few persons are ever confronted with a situation in which a choice must be made between a deeply ingrained custom and an official regulation. When they are confronted with such choices, they do not necessarily behave in a consistent manner. If a man has committed himself to a positivistic philosophy of law, he will probably accept the official regulation; but ordinary men never make such commitments. They are inclined, instead, to judge each case as it comes along and to act according to their interests as they see them at the time. If they believe that no great harm will follow from violation of the official law, they are likely to opt for continued observance of the custom. If the custom is deeply ingrained, they may take grave risks in order to perpetuate what is to them very precious, even though it is condemned by the majesty of the law. And this may be so even where the custom at issue is not connected with religious rites and is not believed to be a moral duty. The unwritten law reigns supreme.

The positivistic approach to law doesn't work because it's wrong. It's too narrow, too restrictive to account for the many legal phenomena with which we are familiar. Its paradoxical inability to locate a sovereign in the United States is no paradox, for the United States is a complex mixture of legal systems—some horizontal and some vertical—with ill-defined, overlapping edges. The legal positivist's conclusion that primitive law and international law do not exist is the unhappy consequence of failing to rec-

ognize that the essence of law is not to be identified either
with its source or with the means by which it is enforced,
but rather with its function—that of regulating the lives
of human beings and the groups into which they form
themselves.

LAW IS WHAT PEOPLE CONCEIVE IT TO BE

There is yet another way in which one may look at
the law: People tend, on the whole, to act in accordance
with what they believe to be the law. The common
man's conception of contract, for example, is quite different from that of the lawyer. If two men, Brown and
Black, make an agreement with one another which each
of them believes to be a legally binding contract, they
will both, in all likelihood, fulfill the conditions of the
agreement—even though a lawyer might tell them that in
reality, the agreement was not legally binding and the
courts would not enforce it. Brown and Black were mistaken in their assumption that the contract was *legally*
binding, for we will say, by hypothesis, that the lawyer's
judgment is decisive on that point. Insofar as the law
of the state is concerned, the contract is a nullity. But
is it not clear that there is an important sense in which
it is not?

Brown and Black act in every respect as if the contract
they had signed were a legally binding contract. Their
actions are governed by their legally null contract every
bit as much as they would be if the contract were
legally enforceable. Each of them performs his end of
the agreement because he believes that he ought to keep
agreements he has made, because he respects the law,
because he fears the consequences of failure to do so—
just as he would if the agreement were legally enforceable.
If one of them should balk at fulfilling one of the conditions to which he had committed himself, the other
might threaten him with legal action, and the threat might
be sufficient to make him live up to his commitments. How,

then, does the "agreement" between Brown and Black differ from one that might have been drawn up by their attorneys? In either case, their actions are identical, their feelings about the agreement are identical, their claims as to their respective rights and duties are identical, even their threats and reactions are identical. Wherein, then, lies the difference?

The only important difference obviously lies in what the courts will do if a suit is brought by one party or the other. If Brown brings suit against Black for Black's alleged failure to live up to his commitments under their "agreement," he will learn to his dismay that no agreement ever existed between him and Black, and that there is no remedy for him in the courts. Black, needless to say, will be as surprised as Brown at this startling— but to him, pleasing—revelation.

Now, is it true that no agreement ever existed between Brown and Black? Does the lawyer's authoritative assurance that the contract is legally invalid mean that there never was a contract? The answer to this question must be a qualified no. The so-called "contract" which Brown and Black drew up shared every important characteristic but one with one that their lawyers might have drawn up. The characteristic which the lawyer's contract would have had that was lacking in Brown and Black's "contract" was enforceability in the courts of law. Therefore, if the question before us is, "Is the contract drawn up by Brown and Black enforceable by the courts?" the answer would have to be *no*. But if the question is, "Is the contract drawn up by Brown and Black a contract?" the answer ought to be *yes, except that it is not enforceable in the courts;* for it has all the characteristics that any other contract has, with that one exception—and that one exception is not enough to justify our refusing to call it a contract.

One might object that to call such a "contract" or "agreement" a *contract* or an *agreement* is to do violence to our language, or to indulge in contradictions, for contracts and agreements are necessarily (that is, by definition) instruments which are enforceable by the courts.

One might also object that the uneducated man who points at the first whale he has ever seen and says, "My, whales are huge fish, aren't they?" is doing violence to our language and is indulging in contradictions, since fish are necessarily (that is, by definition) creatures which have gills, are cold-blooded, have two-chambered hearts, and do not possess mammary glands, while the whale has no gills, is warm-blooded, has a four-chambered heart, and possesses mammary glands. My reply to such pedantry would be the following: To the ordinary man, uninstructed in the technical vocabulary of the zoologist, a fish is a creature which lives in the water, which has paddle-shaped appendages with which it propels itself through the water, and a fish-shaped tail which it uses to steer itself as it swims through the water—as it does all the time. By these criteria, the whale is a fish, though the eel might not be. (The eel might be more closely related to the snake than to the trout, in the ordinary man's scheme of things.)

Now, if I were asked, by a person uninstructed in the technical language of zoology, whether it is not true that a whale is a fish, I would answer either with a qualified *yes* or with a qualified *no*. "Yes," I would say, "the whale is a fish, but you would not pass an exam in zoology if you said so." I might then go on to explain to him some of the technical distinctions which zoologists have found useful in distinguishing one kind of animal from another. But I would be careful to explain to him that this is just the zoologist's way of using the word "fish," and that we ordinary mortals have a perfect right to use it as we have always used it, so long as we remember not to do so in zoology class. Similarly, ordinary mortals have a perfect right to call the instrument which Brown and Black drew up an *agreement* or a *contract*, so long as they are careful not to do so in law school. It is the attorney's duty to point out that such a contract is not enforceable, and that the court will refuse to call it a "contract," since in courts, the word "contract" has a very precise, technical meaning. But in ordinary language, one can say the same thing by calling this instrument an *unenforceable contract* (or an *unenforceable agreement.*)

Now the same thing may be said of "law." *Law is what people conceive it to be.* If people believe that a given rule is a rule of law, if they respect the rights which others claim to have under that rule, if they believe that the rule imposes upon them certain duties and they act upon that belief, if they demand of others that they do likewise, if they treat the rule in every respect as they would treat a rule of law, then *that rule is a rule of law, even though it may not be enforceable in the courts, even though it may never have been passed by any legislature, even though it is not enforced by the police.* To call such a rule a "law" in law school might result in a poor grade for the course. For the lawyer to advise his client on the assumption that such a "law" is a law in his technical sense of the word might result in serious loss to his client and in loss of business for himself. But with the necessary qualifications, there is no reason whatever to refuse to call such a rule a *law.*

CUSTOM IS CONSTITUTIVE OF LAW

In Chapter I, it was noted that "custom" is not univocal, but that a number of related but significantly different kinds of acts can appropriately be called "customs." A similar conclusion was reached in Chapter II with regard to the expression, "source of law." In Chapter III I pointed out how inadequate natural-law theories are, even in their most widely accepted applications, and in the early sections of the present chapter, showed how inadequate positive-law theories are, at least in some important areas.

I have attempted to show that custom serves as a source of law in at least two different senses: as a *cause* (in its effects upon the rulings of judges and the leanings of legislators, to say nothing of the inclinations of their constituencies), and as *evidence* for the existence of law. I rejected the natural-law theorists' contention that a necessary condition for all law is that the natural law serve as at least one of its sources—either in the sense that the particular law must be derivable from the natural law, or in the sense that it must be consistent with it. I also rejected the positivist claim that authority is the source of all law. Finally, I concluded that law is what people conceive it to be, that even where there is no authority invested with the power to pass laws, to enforce them, or to settle disputes, *there is law* just the same, *provided people generally act as if they were following a rule, and provided further that they believe that there is a rule prescribing a certain course of conduct which they feel obliged to follow.*

From this it does not follow that all people act in accordance with the rule or even that all people acknowledge its existence. Nor does it follow that any person follows the rule all the time, or that each person who acknowledges its existence acts in accordance with its dictates on every occasion when strict adherence to the rule would require that he do so. All that is required is that its existence be *generally* acknowledged and that people *regularly* act in accordance with it (in the sense of "regular" that was outlined in Chapter I).

The reader will recognize that the kind of rule I am here describing was defined above as a *practice,* one of the most general types of *custom.*

I am claiming, then, not only that custom is a constituent of law, or that it is a source of law, as most other writers have acknowledged, but that in a very important sense, custom is *constitutive of law;* that is, that some customs *are* laws, in and of themselves. This conception of law may provide a useful corrective to some of the deficiencies of the excessively narrow and restrictive positivistic theories.

In certain areas, the customs of the community, or

"community standards" as they are sometimes called, are explicitly recognized as governing the operation of the law. For example, Mr. Justice Brennan, in the famous case of *Roth* v. *United States,* said that the test of obscenity was "whether to the average person, applying contemporary community standards, the dominant theme of the material taken as a whole appeals to prurient interest."[18] Mr. Justice Harlan, in a later case, argued that such terms as "obscene, lewd, lascivious, indecent, filthy, or vile" must connote "something that is portrayed in a manner so offensive as to make it unacceptable under current community mores."[19] These definitions may be compared to that of the American Law Institute's Model Penal Code: "Material is obscene if, considered as a whole, its predominant appeal is to prurient interest, that is, a shameful or morbid interest, in nudity, sex or excretion, and if in addition it *goes substantially beyond customary limits* of candor in describing or representing such matters."[20] If this definition were to be accepted by the courts—as it has—then the "customary limits of candor" would be definitive in determining whether a given article was obscene. Going beyond those customary limits would be both necessary and sufficient for being obscene under the law. Whether through legislation fashioned after the Model Penal Code, or adjudication based upon the definitions of Justices Brennan and Harlan, custom is recognized as being determinative of law in this instance, and in many others as well.

In order to see how custom can be constitutive of law, I shall adapt a device utilized by Plato in the

[18] 354 U.S., 489.
[19] 370 U.S., 482.
[20] American Law Institute Model Penal Code, Proposed Official Draft (May 4, 1962), Section 251.4 (1). Emphasis mine. For an excellent critique of these definitions and a discussion of the Supreme Court's decisions in the Roth case, the Ginzburg case, and others, see C. Peter Magrath, "The Obscenity Cases: Grapes of Roth," in *The Supreme Court Review* (Chicago: University of Chicago Press, 1966), 7ff. I am indebted to Professor Paul A. Freund for this example.

Republic. There, it will be recalled, Plato wanted to ascertain the nature of the virtue of justice; but in order to find out what justice is on an individual level—in the microcosm, so to speak—he chose to examine it first where it is "writ large," on the level of the state—in the macrocosm. The problem we face here is the reverse. We have trouble recognizing law in the macrocosm, in the relations of states. Let us therefore examine it "writ small," on a microcosmic level which is familiar to all, and turn to the story of an imaginary football game in an imaginary neighborhood told by an imaginary narrator.

THE NEIGHBORHOOD FOOTBALL GAME: A STUDY IN THE GROWTH OF CUSTOMARY LAW

In my neighborhood, when I was a little boy, the boys would get together on a certain day in the fall of the year to play the season's first game of football. No one ever set the date for the first game of the year, but somehow, almost by instinct, every boy in the neighborhood knew when the day had come. This game—or I should say, this series of games—had been played in my neighborhood for generations. The membership on the teams was constantly changing, insofar as actual persons were concerned; but there was a sense in which the membership was static, too. That is, as far back as anyone could remember, there had always been a Kelly, a Goldberg, a Lopez, a Colucci, and so on. The first names always changed, but the last names seldom did.

So far as we could tell, no one had ever made up the rules. For all we knew, they had just grown up by themselves. (Actually, we never thought much about where the rules had come from, anyway.) This was in the days before Little Leagues had been introduced into my town. There were no grownups around to tell us what the rules were—they were all too busy earning their livings in those days to tell kids how to play games. And fathers never came to boss us around, being umpires and referees, breaking up fights and settling arguments. We settled them ourselves, one way or the other.

The interesting thing about our rules, as I was saying, is that although they had grown up by themselves, more or less, I noticed that every now and then there would be little changes in the way we played the game. One time, for example, one boy's eye was poked out by another boy straight-arming him. After that, there was no straight-arming for a long time. No one told us to stop straight-arming, we never got together to take a vote about it, and we certainly never wrote up any agreements about it. We were all horrified by what had happened, and we simply didn't do it any more. It was a very strong rule in our games. Once, I remember, a boy who moved in from out of town started playing on one of our teams. Apparently, where he came from, they straight-armed. But he learned our rule very quickly!

As I have said, there were different ways of settling arguments. One way was quick and easy: If two boys disagreed, they would slug it out and the one who came out on top was right. This always provided a lot of excitement, but it also broke up a lot of friendships, cracked some bones, and ruined many of our games. The worst fights always broke out between the captains of the teams and the referees. It got so bad after a while that nobody wanted to be a referee any more. (The captains were always the biggest ones on the teams.) Since we needed referees for our games, we made up a new rule: Whenever anyone hit a referee, he had to sit out all the games for a week. I remember how we got that rule. One day, after two referees went home crying, we all got together and decided that that was what we would do. After all, according to our rules, everybody had to take a turn being a referee, and nobody wanted to be beaten to a pulp by one of the big guys. So that rule, you might say, was "passed" by all of us—all but the captains, that is. Naturally, they weren't very happy when they heard about it. The first time we had to sideline a captain, he tried to beat up the lot of us; but we stuck together, and it worked. From then on, it was easy.

My father told me that when he was young, the captains used to be rotated, just as we rotated the referees. But one time some big kids simply stayed on after they had become captains, and no one ever challenged them. And that was the end of the rotation rule for captains.

At one time we had a very strict rule about the number of boys who could play on each team. It was always nine. Each member of the team had a certain position and a certain job to do. If there were more, it created problems, and there was no job for the extra men to do. If there were fewer, the teams were in trouble. So we were very strict about it, until one year, when there were two sets of twins, the Franciones and the Bergers. We couldn't take one without the other, and we felt that it wouldn't have been right to split up the twins. So we let each team have an extra member. I don't know how it happened, but somehow, the teams found a job for the extra boy to do, and now, even though there are no twins in the neighborhood, the game is never played with nine boys. The boys now say there have to be ten players, or one of the important positions is left open. I tried to explain to them the way the game is supposed to be played, but they didn't seem to understand. They claimed it was natural to have ten members on the team.

During my freshman year in high school, the whole neighborhood started to change. By the following year, it was no longer recognizable as the same neighborhood. A large number of people moved in from a foreign country. They didn't understand our language, they wore funny clothes, and they had peculiar ways about them. Their boys had played a kind of football wherever they came from, but it was very different from ours. Naturally, when they moved in, they wanted to join our teams. At first we wouldn't let them. We made them be the water boys and do other menial tasks. We said we were training them to play on the team, but really we weren't. Our games had always been played by the Kellys, the Goldbergs, the Lopez boys, the Coluccis, and the other families who lived in our neighborhood. We didn't understand these Kanandas and Yoshitos and Buswanas or want them on the teams.

But finally we had to give in. They got tired of being water boys and threatened to ruin everything if we didn't let them play. So now they've been admitted to the teams. And since then, a strange thing has happened. At first, things went along as they always had, according to our rules, with little changes here and there. But now, with all the foreigners on the team, the game has slowly evolved into something very different from what it was when I was a boy. It simply isn't the same game any more. The boys on the block play the game perfectly well, and they seem to be getting along fairly well together, but it's hard for an old-timer like me to understand what they're doing. For instance, the foreigners, who are quite formal, somehow got the boys on the teams to accept their way of handling disputes. The disputants must shake hands, bow, and smile, and then go before a "commission" of three boys, which listens to their arguments and decides who is right. Sometimes, the boys still slug it out to find out who's right, but in most cases, they go through all this formal rigmarole. It's amazing! I'll never be able to figure out how they got the Kellys, the Goldbergs, the Lopezes, the Coluccis, and the rest to go along with such a rule. I know that if they'd let me take over, I'd set them straight with the old rules, as they're supposed to be—the natural way. But they say they don't want adults telling them how to play. They say they *are* playing according to the old rules, and that the game has *always* been played this way. Ah, me! That's the younger generation for you!

CUSTOMARY LAW APPLIED TO THE LAW OF NATIONS:
A FINAL REPLY TO THE POSITIVISTS

There is no need to spell out all the lessons which are
so easily spotted in this story. It was designed, after all,
specifically for this purpose. I shall confine myself, instead, to a few summary comments.

First, I am well aware of the dangers inherent in
analogical reasoning. Those dangers are stressed in all in-
troductory philosophy courses. I am aware also of the
power of analogical reasoning—a power too often overlooked and minimized in the zeal to demonstrate the
fallacies inherent in the teleological argument.[21] Game
analogies have been very fruitful recently in a number of
fields, including philosophy. I therefore feel no need to
offer further justification for using one here, where rules
of a type not at all distantly related to those of games
are being studied.

Secondly, just as rules of games can come into existence
and be enforced and observed without formal legislation, ad-

---

[21] The teleological argument, it will be recalled, is an attempt,
utilizing analogical reasoning, to prove that God exists. The
most popular version proceeds as follows: If you came across
a watch on a desert island, and observed its complex works and
the intricate way in which all its parts mesh with one another
to make a single, integrated mechanism, you would be unreasonable if you supposed that it had fallen together as a result
of the action of the tides, the sun, and the wind. You would
have to conclude that it was designed by a clever and intelli-
gent artisan. Now if such a comparatively simple mechanism
is compared to an atom, a solar system, or the universe, which
are far more complex and reveal evidence of even more intricate interrelationships, surely it would be unreasonable to
suppose that the watch must have been the product of an in-
telligent designer, but that the atom, the solar system, or the
universe came into existence as the result of some fortuitous
accident. The classic critique of this argument is to be found
in David Hume's *Dialogues Concerning Natural Religion*. Philosophy instructors take special delight in using Hume's arguments to demolish the teleological proof before their freshman
students.

judication, or enforcement, so also can the laws which govern the relations of states to one another. Those who deny that such rules may properly be called *laws* usually mean nothing more than that they have not yet become as clearly defined, as easily enforced, as universally observed, or as rigidly institutionalized as have the civil and criminal laws of most modern states. It is less paradoxical to say simply that international law is not yet clearly defined, easily enforced, and so on.

It isn't difficult to imagine a Hobbesian game theorist insisting that the boys in my story didn't play a *game,* since there can be no game without rules, and they had no *rules.* They had no rules because they had no rule-maker, no rule-enforcer, and no judge to arbitrate disputes, all of which are essential to the existence of rules. On this theory, it turns out that the only boys who have ever played games are those who have been organized into leagues presided over by fathers who codified the rules and saw that they were observed. Though the absurdity of this theory is patent, it seems that the absurdity of the corresponding theory of law is not, and so must be demonstrated.

Finally, consider the sources of international law. A philosopher of law in the Hobbesian or Austinian tradition would insist that only that which is promulgated by a sovereign is law, the assumption being that a necessary condition for the existence of law is its having the decree of a sovereign as one of its sources. It has become obvious that there are many kinds of sources of law, only some of which happen to square with this criterion. The Hobbesian or Austinian might concede that since the courts are agents of the sovereign, their decisions, insofar as they make law, have as their ultimate source the will of the sovereign. But somehow, all other sources whatever they may be, must either be shown to be reducible to the will of the sovereign (as court decisions can), or they must be considered sources only in a secondary sense, not as *lawmaking,* but rather as accidents (in the Aristotelian sense) of law, perhaps as characteristics which may help one understand how the law came to be, but not as essential elements in the making of *law per se*.

But this, too, is unduly restrictive. The boys in the story deliberated about some of the rules by which they played. They voted on others. Some (like the rule about straight-arming) came into existence through the tacit consent of each of them, while others (like the rule requiring ten boys on a team) arose as a result of sheer historical accident, and a grudging concession to temporary conditions; but with the passage of time, this grudging concession was transformed into a rigid rule, sanctioned by current need, which was itself a result of new institutions having arisen to fill the exigencies of the moment; and from the boys' point of view, the rule had the further sanctions of immemorial antiquity (for no one except an interfering grownup—or historian—could remember a time when football teams did not have ten members) and current universal usage.

The laws of nations are very much like the rules of the football game in this respect. They are observed because of veneration for immemorial antiquity and because of the needs and expectations that have arisen from ancient and widespread usage. Though there is no sovereign to legislate for them, to enforce the laws, or to adjudicate disputes, laws nevertheless arise, nations act in accordance with their provisions, and they expect others to do the same. The laws arise in many ways— by express international agreement, usually articulated in treaties (like the sideline rule for boys who hit referees); by tacit consent (like the straight-arming rule) which soon becomes so universally accepted and so strongly binding that one who violates the accepted norm is treated as one might treat a lawbreaker in a civil society (he may be reprimanded or censured, he may be warned against further misbehavior, he may be ordered to make reparation for any damage he may have done, and he may be subjected to such coercion and such sanctions as the community of nations may be able—and willing— to exert); and finally, by usage which may have been engendered by the introduction of temporary expedients (like the "temporary" tenth team member) which gradually give rise to such strong needs and expectations that they become accepted by the community (or—to be more precise—by its members) as binding and as obligatory. Such, then, are some of the sources of international law: express consent by treaty; tacit consent evidenced by permitting others to engage in the practice and by engaging in it oneself; and the unconscious development of expectations, rights, and duties as a result of temporary concessions and expedients originally designed to meet specific, short-term needs and conditions. These latter are sometimes called *customs*.

In international law, we find examples of a number of the various types of custom examined above. Thus, nations may engage in certain practices which would fall under our category of *maxims*. Support of the work of the International Red Cross might fall under this category: Those nations who support the Red Cross do so deliberately, with full awareness of what they are doing, and out of a conviction that they have a duty to do so. But if a nation should choose to withdraw its support of the Red Cross, or refuse to join those who do support it, there are no sanctions that would be leveled against it for so doing, and there is no provision for coercing it into reversing its position.

Other rules of the law of nations more closely resemble *practices*. That is, they more closely resemble purely descriptive rules than those which carry normative or prescriptive force. Thus, for many years it was customary for all nations to send men, not women, as their ambassadors to other nations. No doubt at one time, a breach of this rule would have been regarded with disdain as a breach of diplomatic courtesy; but for some time, it was probably (for the most part) merely a relic of past usage and a result of the failure of qualified women to apply for such posts. Though the nations that engaged in the practice may have done so quite deliberately, they may have felt no particular *duty* to do so; they might have continued the practice, as I say, primarily as a result of inertia, the normal human resistance to change. Nor would their "breach" of the rule necessarily have been visited by sanctions—at least, not by most nations— or by efforts to coerce them into conforming to standard usage. And it was quite within the power of the community of nations to change the rule, simply by doing otherwise.

There are well-known rules of international (or diplomatic) etiquette which closely resemble, in every important respect, the rules of etiquette described above in the chapter on custom. There is no need to go into detail about them here.

And finally, in the customary law of nations, it is not hard to find examples of regulations and of what have been called simple customs. The laws of war are replete with regulations of all kinds. The rule prohibiting seizure of fishing vessels plying their trade in coastal waters has already been cited. This is a rule which has arisen through long and widespread usage. Those who practice it do so deliberately and consciously, out of a conviction that it is wrong to seize such vessels. If a nation fails to abide by the rule, it may be forced, by other nations, to make reparations—and if it is a flagrant violator, it is conceivable (though admittedly unlikely) that sanctions might be invoked against it. And, finally, the rule may be changed by general consent.

There was a time, to be sure, when the law of nations was not justiciable, when the only remedy a nation had for an alleged violation of its rights was the remedy of self-help, when the nations of the world stood literally in a state of nature relative to one another, "in the state and posture of gladiators; having their weapons pointing, and their eyes fixed on one another; that is, their forts, garrisons, and guns upon the frontiers of their kingdoms; and continual spies upon their neighbors; which is a posture of war."[22] But today, though this picture is uncomfortably similar to the view we see all around us,

[22] Hobbes, *Leviathan*, Part I, Chapter xiii.

there is an international court to which nations may bring their disputes for impartial arbitration, and an international body in which disagreements may be aired and in which the agents of governments from all parts of the world may exert their governments' influence to bring the parties in dispute to a peaceable resolution of their differences.[23]

There can be no doubt that there is a law of nations, though it may not be "law" in the Hobbesian sense (in the sense in which a student going to a Hobbesian school would score a correct mark for an affirmative response to the examination question, "Are the relations between the United States and the Soviet Union governed by law?"). The sense in which there *is* a law of nations is much closer to the sense which I have described above —a law which exists in spite of the fact that there is no sovereign whose command it is, no sovereign who will enforce its provisions. Rather, there is a complicated set of laws governing the relations between the nations of the world whose nature is comparable in every important respect to the rules of the neighborhood football game— in their development, in the ways in which they are enforced, and most particularly in the mode of their existence: They exist only insofar as nations believe that they exist, only to the extent that nations are willing to submit themselves to them, only to the degree that nations feel obliged to conduct themselves in accordance with them, only so long as they choose to play the game.

[23] The picture Hobbes draws is, as I have said, too similar to the view we see all around us to permit us to indulge in premature self-congratulation. But the United Nations and the International Court of Justice have undoubtedly brought the world closer to the establishment of meaningful international laws than it has ever been before—meaningful in the sense that they might be established by virtually universal consent, and in the sense that more international disputes are being settled through these peaceful means today than ever before. The process has clearly not developed as far as one would like, but there is room for some satisfaction at those developments which have taken place.

Chapter V

Custom and the Abrogation of Law

THE EFFECTS OF DESUETUDE UPON THE LAW: SUÁREZ'S TREATMENT OF DESUETUDE

Just as custom can create law, so too can it destroy it. And just as there are those who deny that custom can create law, so are there those who deny that it can destroy it. And there are those, too, who adhere to the view that some form of authority is necessarily a source of all law, and hence of the abrogation of any law; and that even though custom may serve as a source of law, or as a source of a law's abrogation, custom alone is never sufficient.

Suárez, for example, says that customs originate in the will or desire of the people, and derive their authority pre-eminently from them and only secondarily from the (usually) tacit consent of the sovereign.[1] I have attempted to show, in the section preceding, that neither the consent of a sovereign nor the sovereign himself is necessary for the establishment of custom.

But suppose that the organs of the state have sanctioned a certain practice, and that that practice has fallen into desuetude. What are the legal effects of such disuse?

[1] Cf. Suárez, op. cit., 562, and 468f.

Suárez says that the principal reason militating against the acceptance of the power of custom to abrogate law is

> that a custom can have no force unless it is reasonable, . . . but a custom, in opposition to law, cannot be reasonable: both because, by the very fact that it is contrary to law, it is against reason; and again because the actions done in pursuance of that custom deviate from right order and cannot work to the favour of those who offend, nor liberate them from the yoke of the law.[2]

Nevertheless, Suárez says that custom may abrogate existing law, both canon and civil, for in his opinion the power to abrogate law rests in the hands of the people; and when they manifest their will, as they do through the observance of customs, their right cannot be denied. Even with respect to canon laws and laws established by a prince, some people say that "these laws are enacted unconditionally, but with the tacit proviso that the people wish to retain them in force,"[3] so that there is built into such laws the stipulation that they may be abrogated by the people. Suárez himself does not accept this assumption, for in his opinion, both the prelates of the Church and temporal princes have the power to bind their subjects unconditionally. However, as a result of "a union of the people with their prince and lawmaker," i.e., an act on the part of the people and toleration and consent to that act on the part of the lawmaker, a law may be put aside. Thus, a custom may not abrogate a law in those states which are ruled by a sovereign prince or in the Church, unless there is at least tacit approval and consent on the part of the authorities. In such cases, the community does not possess an "active power" of making or repealing law; it has only the power to establish a custom contrary to the existing law, which custom then

2 Ibid., 590.
3 Ibid., 591.

constitutes a demand by the community that the superior exercise his authority to abolish the law.[4] However, the establishment of a positive custom is not the only way in which a community may manifest its will to abrogate any existing law. A second way is for the community to establish what Suárez calls a "privative" custom; that is, by repeatedly omitting to perform acts which they are legally bound to perform, the members of the community allow the law to fall into desuetude, and when this is done deliberately, it is a clear indication of the community's desire that the law in question be abrogated.[5]

As an interesting corollary to this, it follows that for a time, those persons who disobey the positive law, either by failing to obey a positive injunction and allowing it to fall into desuetude, or by violating a negative injunction, are committing crimes and are "necessarily sinful."

Some authorities, disagreeing both with this last conclusion and with the objection which has been offered to the possibility of custom abrogating law, argue that when the need arises, human law may properly be disobeyed, and that if such occasions should arise frequently, a custom contrary to the original law would be established, indicating strongly that the original law was not advantageous to the community, and thus abrogating it.[6] Suárez's reply to this is that it does not meet the difficulty, for since such acts are not, in fact, contrary to law, and since their accompanying circumstances are such as to evince no intention on the part of the people which might be construed as being opposed to the law, they cannot actually establish a custom contrary to the law. Indeed, if such occasions arise frequently, the law is *ipso facto* shown to be useless, and is abrogated simply "because it has been proved to be burdensome and of no

[4] Ibid., 592.
[5] Ibid., 593.
[6] St. Thomas Aquinas, *Summa Theologica,* Qu. 97, Art. 3, cited in Suárez, 605. Others who share this opinion are cited there.

effect," and not because of the establishment of a contrary custom.[7]

Suárez admits that at the outset, the actions which establish a custom may be bad in that they are in violation of law. Indeed, if such actions are to establish a custom which will have the effect of abrogating law, "they will inevitably be bad at the outset because they are in opposition to a law which is binding, and this, apart from any excuse or plea of ignorance."[8] In spite of this, however, such acts may ultimately result in the abrogation of law; for their long-run effects are not evil, and in fact they may eventually be lawful (after abrogation of the law).

Nevertheless, one might urge that since the law that was abolished was reasonable (for if it were not, it could never have been established in the first place), the opposing custom must therefore be unreasonable, not only because it has been introduced by unlawful acts, but also because it tends to abolish a reasonable law.[9] But if this argument were valid, it would also hold against the express abrogation of a law; and it is clear that such abrogation may be both reasonable and just. The problem arises from an ambiguity in the word "reasonable." In one sense, it may refer to that which is *necessary*, and in the other to that which is *suited to bringing about certain effects*. In other words, according to Suárez, some things are intrinsically reasonable, others are so only instrumentally. In many cases, either of two alternatives may bring about desirable effects. Hence, even though the original law may be reasonable in that it has certain beneficial results, its contrary, established by custom, may also be reasonable in that it will have other beneficial results. Thus, Suárez says, there is no philosophical justification for denying that custom is a source of law. It is, both in the positive sense of establishing new law where

[7] Suárez, op. cit., 606.
[8] Ibid., 607.
[9] Ibid., 607f.

there was none before, and in the negative sense of abrogating old law.

Suárez's conclusion that a custom that is contrary to law is *ipso facto* against reason is based upon the premise that the law is necessarily reasonable, which is another way of saying that it is consistent with the natural law. Sufficient consideration to the "conformity to reason" criterion for law has already been given above, in the discussion of the natural law.

As for Suárez's second point, there are those who would consider it to be well taken. From one point of view, at least, we ought not to countenance anyone's violating the law, even when he does so with the intention of abrogating, through his acts, a law with whose provisions he is not in sympathy. On this view, such actions are a form of anarchy, and allowing the law to be changed by such methods constitutes a reward for the lawbreaker's lawlessness. It is not an orderly method for bringing about legal reforms.

However, much as we may deplore lawbreaking in general, there are clearly specific instances in which the only right thing to do is to break the law. In the United States, for example, if one has the conviction that a certain ordinance is unconstitutional, one need not wait for the law to be changed by the cumbersome and often stubbornly conservative processes of legislation or the more uncertain process of change through the ballot box. One may instead challenge the law by openly violating it, inviting arrest, and carrying an appeal through the courts. This is a perfectly legitimate method, so long as one is prepared to accept the consequences of defeat.

In addition, new problems have arisen with the attempt by some individuals and groups to bring the public to an awareness of allegedly unjust laws by carrying on unlawful demonstrations. This is a very difficult and complicated problem, far beyond the scope of the present study. But the very difficulty of the problem points up the inadequacy of such simplistic solutions as those of

Suárez and those who uncritically insist that law and order must be maintained at all costs. Surely this is not true. There are other values which must also be maintained. We must not allow ourselves to be blinded to them by our concern for the preservation of law and order. No approach to law is more certainly self-defeating.

DESUETUDE RESULTS IN ABROGATION OF LAW

If one accepts the proposition—as I think one must —that in certain senses, custom is a source of law, one must accept the further proposition that custom can abrogate law. For the establishment of any law is the abrogation of another. In order to show that this is so, let me demonstrate what the effects of abrogation of a law are.

AN ANALYSIS OF "ABROGATION OF LAW"

It will be helpful, for the present purpose, to review briefly certain legal relations that were most clearly marked off by W. N. Hohfeld in his *Fundamental Legal Conceptions*.[10] Hohfeld found that the word "right," when it is used in legal contexts, is susceptible of a number of different interpretations, each of which has rather different legal implications. Since I am using Hohfeld's analysis for illustrative purposes only, I shall confine my discussion to only two of these senses of "right."

Let it be assumed that the shells on Elsinore Beach are very valuable, bringing high prices in hobby shops and at auctions. Now consider each of the following statements:

[10] First printed 1913. Reprinted by Yale University Press (New Haven), 1964. An excellent summary and review of Hohfeld's fundamental legal conceptions may be found in Julius Stone, *Legal System and Lawyers' Reasonings* (Stanford, California: Stanford University Press, 1964), 137ff.

(A) Harris has a right to gather seashells on Elsinore Beach.

(B) Harris has a right to the seashells gathered on Elsinore Beach.

There is a variety of circumstances in which these statements might be true.

(A) would be true if any of the following states of affairs prevailed:

(1) Harris has purchased Elsinore Beach and all property rights are vested in him.

(2) Gerber has purchased Elsinore Beach, but has given Harris unrestricted permission to gather shells on it.

(3) Elsinore Beach is in the public domain, and is owned by no one.

(B), however, would be true if (1) were the case, but not if (2) or (3) were the case. (It would be true under (2) only if Gerber had given Harris *exclusive* permission to gather shells on the beach.)

The right described in (B) is called by Hohfeld a *demand-right*. Wherever one person, *X,* has a *demand-right,* some other person (or persons), *Y,* has a corresponding duty. Thus, in the case presently before us, if Harris owns Elsinore Beach, all the shells found thereon belong to him, unless he chooses to give them away or to transfer his rights in them in some other way (as by selling them). He has a right to demand that Gerber turn over to him any shells he may have picked up on Elsinore Beach, or that he compensate him for their loss if he has disposed of them or destroyed them. Gerber, on the other hand, has a duty to refrain from collecting shells on Elsinore Beach, and a duty to return to Harris any shells he may have picked up there. And in this case, what is true of Gerber is true of every other person. Furthermore, Harris's rights in this matter are enforceable in the courts.

To be more specific, (B) means that:

(B_1) Every person has a duty to refrain from gathering shells on Elsinore Beach.

(B_2) Every person has a duty to refrain from removing,

destroying, or in any other way disposing of the shells of Elsinore Beach.

(B_3) Every person has a duty to return to Harris any shells he may have removed from Elsinore Beach, or to compensate him for them.

There is yet another duty bound up with this relationship which neither Hohfeld nor any of the persons who have commented on his "fundamental legal conceptions" has previously mentioned:

(B_4) The court having jurisdiction over Elsinore Beach has a duty to enforce the duties listed above.

I shall assume, that is, that the right-duty relationship is not diadic, but triadic, and that it is to be outlined as follows:

If (C) X has a demand-right over Y, then,

(D) Y has a duty toward X, and

(E) the court having jurisdiction over X and Y has a duty to X to uphold his demand-right over Y, or (what amounts to the same thing)

(E_1) the court has duty to X to compel Y to fulfill his duty toward X. The court also has

(E_2) a demand-right toward Y that he fulfill his duty to X. X accordingly has also

(C_1) a demand-right over the court that it uphold his demand-right over Y; and Y has

(D_1) a duty to the court to obey its command that he fulfill his duty toward X.

I am suggesting that Hohfeld and those who have followed him have overlooked an important set of legal relations, namely, the relations existing between parties to a dispute and the courts. I do *not* want to suggest, however, that *all* legal relations are triadic—that is, all legal relations in the broad construction of the term, a construction which (as the reader knows) I am concerned to show is unable to accommodate whole areas of the law. (The contract drawn up by Brown and Black establishes a diadic legal relation—in the broad sense of "legal"—but no legal relation in the narrow Austinian sense. The contract drawn up by their attorneys establishes a triadic legal relation in *both* senses.[11]) No legal relation in the narrow sense is not triadic.

One might argue that the triadic relationship cannot apply to all legal relations in the narrow sense, since that would entail an infinite regress. If all demand-right-duty relationships are enforceable by a court, what of the demand-right-duty relationship existing between X and the court (E and C_1)? One might reply that if the court fails to fulfill its duty toward X, X may appeal to a higher court which will order the lower court to fulfill the duty it had previously shirked. But this suggests that the higher court must have a duty to X, relative to X's relations with the lower court. There must now be a still higher court which will enforce the second court's duty to enforce the lower court's duty—and so on *ad infinitum*. If there is a supreme court, beyond which there is no appeal, we must conclude either that the supreme court has no legal duties, since there is no higher court to which one can appeal (and this is precisely the conclusion that Hobbes reached, when he said, in *Leviathan*, that the sovereign owes no duties toward his subjects, since there can be no contract between them, seeing that there is no one over both of them to enforce such a "contract"), or that the relationship existing between X and the supreme court is not a legal relationship. Either of these conclusions is paradoxical in the extreme. The solution to the paradox is to be found in the broader conception of law (and hence of legal duties) I am advocating. The supreme court has legal duties, and the relationship between X and the supreme court is a legal relationship in spite of the fact that there is no higher court to enforce these duties, for law consists of what people (including judges) conceive it to be, and is determined by their practices; it is not dependent upon an enforcing agency except in extraordinary circumstances.

But from this it does not follow that the triadic relationship does not hold in every legal relationship (in

[11] See *supra*, 120f.

the narrow sense). It shows only that the narrow sense of "legal relationship" is so restrictive as to cut off certain perfectly respectable and highly important legal relationships.

Returning now to Harris, Gerber, and the shells on Elsinore Beach, let us examine (A), Harris's right to gather shells on the beach. In order to simplify matters, let us assume that Gerber would like to put an end to Harris's shell-gathering business. If we assume that all of Gerber's efforts to induce Harris voluntarily to stop gathering shells have failed, then his options are reducible to two: exercising force upon Harris to prevent him from gathering shells, or asking the courts to issue an injunction against future shell-gathering by Harris.

Under any of the conditions (1), (2), or (3) above, Harris has a demand-right against Gerber's forcibly preventing him from gathering shells, and Gerber has a corresponding duty to refrain from exerting such force against Harris; furthermore, the courts will protect Harris's right not to be molested by issuing appropriate injunctions against such acts on the part of Gerber and by punishing him, if necessary.

But let us consider the second possibility. Will the courts uphold Gerber's demand that Harris refrain from gathering the shells on Elsinore Beach?

In none of the situations (1), (2), or (3) will they do so. For in each of those cases, Harris may legally gather the shells on Elsinore Beach if he chooses to do so. He may also refrain from gathering them, if he should so choose. Hohfeld calls such a right a *privilege-right*. Unlike a *demand-right*, a *privilege-right* entails no corresponding *duty* on the part of any other person. It does entail what Hohfeld calls a *no-right*—or, to be more explicit, a *no-demand-right* on the part of others. If Harris has the *privilege-right* of gathering shells on Elsinore Beach, Gerber has *no right to demand* either that he gather them or that he refrain from gathering them. A privilege-right, then, is the absence of a duty, and a no-right is the absence of a demand-right.

Now what of the third element in the triad, the court? Suppose Gerber goes to court seeking an injunction to restrain Harris from gathering shells on Elsinore Beach, and suppose that because of (1), (2), or (3) prevailing, Harris has a privilege-right to gather shells there. The court would then have the duty to refrain from granting Gerber's request, or (what amounts to the same thing) to uphold Harris's privilege-right to gather shells. In other words, Harris has the right to demand (i.e., a *demand-right*) that the court refrain from interfering with his shell-gathering operations, and Gerber has no right (i.e., a *no-right*) to demand that it interfere with Harris's shell-gathering.

With this introduction behind us, let us see now what happens (a) when a law is passed, and (b) when a law is abrogated.

(a) When a law is passed (or when it comes into existence in any other way), a change in legal relations takes place. The passage of a law confers rights where there were none before, or it imposes duties or liabilities or disabilities where there were none before. (For our purposes, there is no need to enter into Hohfeld's other legal relations; the demand-right-duty and privilege-right-no-right relationships will serve as illustrations.) Thus, suppose that (3) had prevailed from time immemorial—that Elsinore Beach had always been in the public domain, and that all persons therefore had the privilege-right of gathering shells there. Suppose, however, that a law is passed conferring upon Harris and Harris alone the right to gather shells at Elsinore Beach. Where before Harris had a privilege-right to gather shells there, he now has a demand-right as well; for he may demand that all other persons refrain from all shell-gathering operations. Where before Gerber had a privilege-right to gather shells there, he now has no privilege-right; instead, he has a duty to refrain from gathering shells. Where before Harris had a no-right with respect to Gerber's shell-gathering, he now has a demand-right.

(b) Suppose now that the law discussed immediately

above (which we shall hereafter call *L*) is abrogated.
Now everything is as it was before the passage of *L*.
It may seem that there is no law, just as there was no
law before. But I shall maintain that there is an important sense in which there *is* a law, and that the
abrogation of *L* is equivalent to the passage of a new
law, *M*.

Let me return for a moment to the situation that
prevailed while *L* was in force. In the discussion of the
legal relations that *L* brought into being, the third element of the triadic relationships that were brought into
being, the courts, was overlooked. Under *L,* the courts
had a duty to enforce Harris's demand-right over Gerber
(and all other persons) by restraining Gerber's attempts
to gather shells, by respecting Harris's demand that Gerber be prevented from gathering shells on Elsinore Beach.

How has the situation changed now that *L* has been
abrogated? Now Gerber has a privilege-right too, and
Harris has a *no-right* with respect to Gerber's shell-
gathering. That is, in effect, the courts now have a duty
to *refrain* from respecting Harris's demand that Gerber
be prevented from gathering shells on Elsinore Beach.

Let me summarize the court's duties under *L* and
no-L:

Under *L:* The court has a duty to respect Harris's demand that Gerber refrain from gathering shells on Elsinore Beach.

Under *no-L:* The court has a duty to *refrain* from
respecting Harris's demand that Gerber refrain from
gathering shells on Elsinore Beach (by dismissing his plea
for an injunction).

Now this result may be obtained in another way.
Suppose the legislature, instead of abrogating *L,* had
passed *M* instead; and suppose that *M* conferred upon
Gerber (and upon everyone else) the right to gather shells
on Elsinore Beach. If such a law were passed, the court
would have had a duty to refrain from respecting Harris's
demand that Gerber refrain from gathering shells on

Elsinore Beach (by dismissing his plea for an injunction), just as it did after the abrogation of L.

In other words, the abrogation of L is identical in its effects with the passage of M. The same may be said of the abrogation (or passage) of any other law. The abrogation of any law is equivalent to the passage of some other law, and (of course) conversely.

Suppose, for example, that M is abrogated. This would be equivalent to the passage of a law imposing a duty upon Gerber (and others) to refrain from gathering shells on Elsinore Beach. Since the absence of a privilege-right entails the presence of a duty, one may take away Gerber's privilege-right by passing a law imposing a duty upon him, by passing a law specifying that he shall no longer have the privilege-right, or by abrogating the law which conferred the privilege-right upon him. These are all equivalent.

Whether the law is silent about shell-collecting, or explicitly grants a permission (or right) to everyone to gather shells where there was no law before, is of no material consequence. But where there has been a demand-right, with its correlative duties, the abrogation of the law granting that demand-right, or the passage of a new law nullifying the duties (granting the privilege) has a material effect. And where there has been no law, or where the law has explicitly permitted shell-collecting, then the abrogation of the law in the latter case, and the passage of a law granting demand-rights or imposing duties in the former, also has a material effect, opposite to that of the actions described in the sentence immediately preceding.

My conclusion, then, is that the establishment of any law is equivalent to the abrogation of a correlative law, and (obviously) the abrogation of any law is equivalent to the establishment of its correlative. Now, if this is granted, and if we grant the proposition that custom can establish law, then it follows that custom can also abrogate law; for the establishment of any law is the abrogation of its correlative.

AN ANALYSIS OF "DESUETUDE"

Desuetude is substitution of one kind of act for another, the establishment of one set of expectations for another, the replacement of one set of customary rights and duties by another. There is no material difference between *custom* and *desuetude,* except that the latter has certain negative connotations while the former has positive ones. When we speak of *custom,* we have in mind a practice that is already established and in general use. When we speak of a practice (or a law) falling into desuetude, we think of a once established practice having fallen into disuse, of a set of expectations which once existed existing no more. But is custom different from law in this respect? Is the "abrogation" of a custom (i.e., its falling into desuetude) not identical with the establishment of a new custom?

A simple example for the sake of illustration—one gleaned not from customary law, but from ordinary, non-legal forms of customs—should be helpful.

As noted above, among certain persons, it is customary for the salad to be served to each guest at the table individually, but in these days of expensive and untrained domestic help, most of the members of that class have acceded to the exigencies of the times and are allowing guests (or, more correctly, *expecting* their guests) to help themselves from large serving bowls filled with salad. One can easily imagine this condition prevailing for a very long time to come—for so long, in fact, that one day an expert on etiquette will write that it is proper to serve salad thus, explaining that the rationale behind the custom is to be found in the fact that guests with peptic ulcers are thereby enabled to take only a small amount of salad, thus avoiding the difficult choice of leaving a large amount on their plates or risking an ulcer attack. (After reading a book of etiquette, one will see that this is not at all farfetched.)

This may all be described in terms very similar to those describing changes in the laws. In the old days, the proper hostess was expected to have her servants serve the salad between the entrée and the dessert; in a very clear sense, she had a *duty* or an *obligation* to do so, and her guests had a demand-right that they be so served. These rights differed from the legal demand-right discussed above in that no court of law would enforce them; but there is a "court of custom," much less formal than any court of law, with less exact procedures. The "court of custom," informal as it is, is in many ways far more effective than any court of law, more exacting in its demands, less merciful in passing judgments, and more ruthless in executing its penalties.

Now, with changed conditions, the hostess has an option: She may have her servants serve salad in accordance with the old custom, or she may have her guests help themselves. She now has a privilege-right, and they have the corresponding no-right. In the informal "court of custom," no sanctions will be visited upon her, whether she chooses to follow the one course or the other.

But on publication of the latest authoritative edition of the rules of etiquette, with the canonization of the new "help yourself" rule, a new demand-right-duty relationship will have been established, with the content of the rule significantly different from what it had been previously.

What has happened is precisely parallel to what happens when a law is abrogated or is replaced by one substituting for a demand-right-duty relationship, a privilege-right-no-right relationship. In place of one custom there is another, and as the first falls into complete desuetude, the second comes into greater prominence.

Another simple example: For several decades it has been customary for men *not* to wear beards, though there was a time, not so very long ago, when it was customary for men to wear beards. This pair of customs probably fits best in the rubric of *simple custom* above, though it may also be considered under the rules of

etiquette. In the transitional period, a man could sport a
beard or appear clean-shaven, as he pleased. How might
the situation during that period best be described?

(1) There was no custom governing men's shaving
habits.

(2) It was customary for men to do as they pleased
about their beards.

I would suggest that it is a matter of indifference
whether one chooses one mode of expression or the other.
They both boil down to the same thing.

But, it might be objected, it makes no sense to speak of
there being a custom allowing men to do just what they
please. Furthermore, there is no sense, among all those
enumerated above, in which "custom" can be shown to
apply to this kind of situation; for "custom" refers in
every case to classes of actions which are performed
regularly, and here, by hypothesis, we're referring to two
classes of actions (shaving and not shaving), neither of
which is performed regularly.

My reply to this is as follows: First, if the statement
has a use in ordinary language, it must make sense; and
it *does* have such a use, for (2) might very easily be
employed by a person wanting to describe the state of
affairs prevailing during that transitional period; no one
would have the slightest trouble understanding what was
meant by it.

Secondly, an analogous situation exists with respect to
the law. It was pointed out above that whether one said
that a law granting a demand-right to Harris was abrogated, or that a law taking away his demand-right was
passed, was a matter of indifference. The proposition that
there is *no law* governing Harris's rights in this matter is
logically identical with the proposition that there *is a law*
conferring a no-right upon him (or denying a demand-
right to him, or giving a privilege-right to everyone).
One might raise the same objection here—that surely
there must be a difference between there being a law and
there being no law. And here the answer is easily discovered. These statements are really elliptical ways of

describing the actions of *courts and their agents*. When we say that there is no law governing Harris's rights in this matter, what we mean—from a pragmatic point of view—is that if he attempts to have the courts interfere with Gerber's shell-collecting, he will be unsuccessful, for the courts will not interfere with Gerber's, or anyone else's, seashell-collecting. When we say that there is a law conferring a privilege-right upon everyone, we mean (in the same sense) the very same thing, for such a law simply directs the courts not to interfere with anyone's seashell-collecting.

Now some statements about custom can be interpreted in an analogous way. They too are elliptical, and we must consider what the pragmatic meaning of each statement is. Turning our attention to (1), then, we find that it means that there was no regularity so far as men's shaving habits were concerned. But from this it can be inferred that there was one regularity. Just as the existence of no law on a given subject assures us that the law courts will regularly ignore or dismiss cases that are concerned with that subject, so also the existence of no custom on men's shaving habits assures us that the "court of custom," sometimes called the "court of public opinion," regularly dismisses any questions that may be brought before it on that matter and refuses to impose sanctions upon men who do wear beards and upon men who don't. Turning our attention to (2), we find that it means the very same thing: The subject of the custom is not men's beards, but the general public's way of treating the subject of men's beards. And the public is quite regular in its treatment of men's beards: It ignores them. Another way of writing (2), then, would have been, "People had the custom of not concerning themselves over whether a man wore a beard or not." To show that this is a custom, like any other, it should be noted that like many customs, this one might have had sanctions joined to it. If it had, people would have been shocked and annoyed if anyone had made fun of a man's shaven (or unshaven) physiognomy, or had attempted to impose social sanctions upon those who did (or upon those who did not) wear beards. They might very well have imposed informal sanctions (of the type reserved for such cases) upon him for being so boorish.

Desuetude, then, is most easily understood as the substitution of one custom for another, though one may look upon it differently if one chooses to do so. In any case, though, it is useful to note what happens when a custom falls into desuetude. A new set of practices inevitably arises, and where rights, duties, expectations, and sanctions are involved, they are transferred elsewhere, just as they are when laws are changed (or abrogated, if you will).

Nothing I have said here should be construed to imply that custom cannot exist without an "informal court." The illustration has been chosen deliberately to show how closely comparable custom and law can be. But the two are comparable in other ways as well. Just as there can be customs which are unenforceable and sanctionless, so also can there be laws which are neither enforced nor sanctioned.

A REPLY TO SUÁREZ'S THEORY THAT TOLERATION AND CONSENT OF THE SOVEREIGN ARE NECESSARY FOR DESUETUDE ABROGATING LAW

Without toleration and consent on the part of the prince, desuetude does not have the power to abrogate law, according to Suárez. The Church and the prince have the right to bind the people unconditionally, he says, but there is a "union" of the people and the prince such that the prince may "tolerate and consent [to]" their customs, even when the latter conflict with his laws. In this way, he attempts to preserve his view that law must emanate from the prince while still accounting for the phenomenon of the abrogation of law through desuetude.

On the theory I have propounded above, it is not necessary to suppose that there is either toleration or consent on the part of the state for either the establishment of law or its abolishment. Toleration and consent are both conscious acts or states of mind. "Jones consented to his daughter's request" presupposes Jones's having been asked for his consent. A necessary precondition for anyone's consenting to anything is that he be asked first for his consent. "Jones tolerates his daughter's boy friend" presupposes Jones's knowing about his daughter's boy friend. One does not tolerate that of which one is unaware. One is simply unaware of it. Toleration implies dislike, and one can dislike only those persons, acts, and things which one believes to exist. It is in the nature of things that many acts are performed of which the officers of the state are totally unaware. Being unaware of them, they do not tolerate them. Nor have they consented to them, since their consent has never been sought. But the acts take place, the laws are laxly enforced or go completely unenforced, and years later someone notices an old statute on the books, long since forgotten, and calls for the removal of dead wood from the laws of the state. The mere presence of some words in a lawbook, stating that so-and-so is forbidden, or that such-and-such is permitted, is no guarantee that so-and-so is forbidden or that such-and-such is permitted. The latter is the case only if there is a living law, actually practiced by the people, conforming to their expectations, their demands, and their needs. Placing the words in the books can have tremendous effects upon the people, as noted above. It can galvanize them into action, raise or lower their expectations, create or crush their demands, fulfill their needs or leave them unfulfilled. It can be woven into the warp and woof of their lives and so become a part of the living law, or it may be locked out of their hearts and thus remain no more than cold words in the lawbooks, preserved for the legal scholar and the historian but entering not at all into the real fabric of society. Though it would be a mistake to underestimate the power of the state insofar as the making of law is concerned, it would also be a mistake to overestimate it.[12]

[12] See Appendix C.

Chapter VI

Toward a Broader Conception of Law

Whatever I may have said above about unduly narrow constructions of the concept of law must now be qualified in the interests of balance and accuracy. There is a virtue in the positivists' concept of law, provided it is not taken so seriously that all broader conceptions of this immensely rich concept are automatically excluded. For some purposes, it is useful to restrict the meaning of "law." If the lawyer were to think of law in terms of the paragraphs immediately preceding, he would soon be out of business. His main concern is, and should be, the law as it is interpreted by the judges. Other persons, with other interests, see the law from other points of view. In what way, then, can custom be said to be a source of law?

The answer must be dependent upon the view we take of the law. Let us look at it, for a moment, through the eyes of the lawyer—of J. C. Gray, for example, who was one of the most articulate spokesmen of the American realist movement. So far as Gray was concerned, the law *is* what judges say it is.[1]

It may be asked what the sources of the law as judges interpret it are. As has been indicated in the chapter on the sources of law, some of these sources are statutes,

[1] John Chipman Gray, *The Nature and Sources of the Law*, *passim*.

parliamentary or congressional or other legislative enact-
ments, and judicial precedents. But one cannot overlook
the historical antecedents, the psychological conditioning of
the judges, their ethical predispositions, the deep-rooted
expectations and dispositions of the people as these are
seen by the judges, and long-standing practice—all of
these factors, and perhaps others as well, converge and
interact with one another in the forming of a judicial
decision. The courts are wont to frame their decisions in
such a way that it appears that nothing but the facts of
the immediate case and purely "legal" considerations
(such as statutes and precedents) have entered into the
making of the decision. Like so much else in the law, this
is a fiction—a useful and honorable one, to be sure, but a
fiction nonetheless.

Since I am not concerned here with delving into the
judicial psyche (others are far more qualified to undertake
that task), I shall let this stand as my account of the way
in which decisions are made. Let it be noted, however, that
in spite of the best efforts put forth by the courts to
conceal (with the noblest intentions!) the workings of
these "non-legal" considerations, there is ample evidence
in court decisions that they do operate and that the judges
are themselves aware of their effects upon them. Here
again, decisions in the hard cases are the best tests, particularly where morals and community standards are
affected, as in civil rights cases, obscenity cases, and cases
involving indecency and such crimes as "conspiracy to
corrupt the public morals."[2]

To say that custom is a source of *all* law, whether it be
judge-made or otherwise, would be overly simplistic, or
would be to expand the meaning of "custom" so widely
that it would include everything and thus become vacuous.
On the contrary, some laws are passed and enforced

[2] On all of this, but particularly on the last mentioned, cf.
H. L. A. Hart, *Law, Liberty and Morality* (London: Oxford
University Press, 1963), *passim*. Note especially the discussion
of the case of *Shaw* v. *Director of Public Prosecutions*, 7ff. *et
passim*.

which have only the remotest connection with the practice of the people, and even with the prior practices of the courts. Many of these deal with highly technical matters which seldom arise except in unusual circumstances. In spite of all that has been said above, some laws are enacted and enforced even though they run *directly counter* to the then prevailing practice of the people. This may be done by well-meaning legislators and judges with the intention of changing the direction of public practice, of *reforming the prevailing custom*. But even here, there is a sense in which the custom has served as a source of the law; for if the practice now outlawed had not existed, or had not been so widespread and caused such disaffection in the community, the legislators would not have felt the need to pass the law, the cases would never have come before the courts, the judges would not have felt compelled to provoke public displeasure by rendering what they undoubtedly knew would be unpopular and possibly even inflammatory verdicts. There is an old rule in historical scholarship that whenever one finds mention of an ordinance or law in ancient sources, it is safe to assume that whatever the law forbade was widespread in that community; for if the practice had not been widespread, no one would have bothered to enact the law. Custom is a source of law at least in the sense that it is a historical antecedent for many laws. The prevailing custom, together with certain feelings of moral revulsion on the part of the lawmakers, or considerations of the public order and welfare, may be sufficient to cause the lawmakers to enact a law designed to bring an end to the custom.

In other cases, where custom has run strongly counter to the then prevailing law (in the narrow, technical sense of "law"), the law has had to change as a result of the supplanting power of custom, either by ceasing to be enforced or by legislative or judicial decree. The particular course that is followed depends upon the procedures most widely accepted in the community. In some communities, the various procedures work side by side, while in others, greater use is made of one method than of another.

Whether the change comes about as a result of lax enforcement, legislative enactment, or judicial interpretation, the effect is the same: The law has been changed, to reflect the prevailing practice in the community. Or, to be more precise, the law—in the technical sense of the word—has been brought into consonance with the law—in the broader sense of the term discussed above.

What emerges from this study, then, is a broader conception of law than has been hitherto available, a conception which is not opposed to the positivist or the realist view, but is rather co-ordinate with them. The positivist and realist concepts of law are useful when one's interest is narrowly focused upon one or another aspect of law. Neither of them is capable of giving an adequate account of the hardest cases—of the force and efficacy of the unwritten law, of international law, of primitive law, or of the effects of desuetude upon the law.

Custom may not only serve as a source of law in several different senses, but also if custom is construed as being constitutive of law, one can account for all the hard cases enumerated above. "Custom," like "law," is a family-resemblance concept. In some senses, "custom" and "law" are compatible with one another, while in others they are incompatible. Comparing and contrasting them in all their manifold complexity, we find that in some areas they may be assimilated to one another, while in others, they may not. If the criminal law be compared with rules of etiquette, for example, parallels in virtually every important aspect of each of them will be found. But a comparison of the criminal law with maxims or the most minimal type of practice reveals some similarities, and many dissimilarities.

One should not suppose, then, that the study of custom will answer every question we may have about the law. But through the broader conception of law propounded in this study, we are able to answer a number of questions which have hitherto been met with perplexity and confusion.

Chapter VII
Conclusion

In this study, we have come a long way from the patronizing and simplistic view that is given expression in the saying that primitive man is a slave to custom. If a native of New Guinea could observe the extent to which our lives are ruled by (for example) the rules of etiquette, he would no doubt be shocked by the extent to which we submit to the hegemony of custom. To him, the elaborate rules governing table manners (to take only one area in which our lives are regulated) might appear to be foolish, trivial, even barbarous and cruel. (Who has not seen a mother scold her child for holding his fork incorrectly? The consequences of violation of the rules of custom can be brutal.) We too are slaves to custom, but we seldom acknowledge the fact, since we believe, usually, that the "customary" way of doing things is the *natural* way of doing things; and "natural" here is used, not as a descriptive term, but as a normative one—the *natural* way of doing things being by definition the *right* way.

And, of course, this is true—by definition. Custom *does* determine what is right and wrong, just as it reflects what people believe to be right and what they believe to be wrong. In this way it enters into our conceptions of moral right and wrong and raises questions in the minds of moral philosophers about the relativity of morals. For clearly,

just as the custom of one time and place is not that of
another, so also moral right and wrong differ from place
to place and from time to time.

Anthropologists and sociologists have been quarreling
for some time over the question, "Are custom and law
in primitive societies to be identified?" As this study
has demonstrated, in certain important significations of the
terms, custom and law are to be identified even in the
most advanced societies. As William Seagle put it in his
book on the history of law, custom is king.

In this study, an attempt has been made to show how
custom is related to law in a great variety of ways: how it
serves as a source of law in the sense that it acts as a kind
of efficient cause, in Aristotle's terminology, and serves as
evidence pointing the way toward the law for judges seeking to find out what the law actually is. Most important,
however, is the conclusion that custom may be regarded
as being constitutive of law, and how that conception
remedies the deficiencies of positivistic and realistic theories of law in accounting for the existence of primitive law,
international law, and the unwritten law, to say nothing of
constitutional law, which cannot easily be accounted for
on at least the positivist theory.

In my analysis, I have attempted to show the great
variety in the kinds of custom, and I have offered some
suggestions as to criteria which may be employed to
distinguish one from another. I have attempted also to
analyze the term "source of law" in order to see in what
ways custom may be considered a source of law, and for
the interest inherent in that difficult and much discussed
subject.

In my discussion of the natural-law theory, I argued
that appeal to the natural law serves no useful purpose
if the natural law is interpreted normatively; and that if
the natural law is interpreted descriptively, there is no
ground for believing that there is such a thing, and some
ground for believing that there is not. I proposed there a
solution to the dilemmas faced by those who must decide
what to do in the face of laws which they conceive to be

iniquitous and in cases where they are confronted with the problem of whether to punish persons who have committed iniquitous acts under color of law.

In the course of that discussion, I considered the relations between law and morals, custom and morals, and custom and law insofar as priorities are concerned, and found that where a negative moral prohibition comes into conflict with either a customary or a legal rule, the moral law is generally considered to take precedence. But if the conflict is between a customary or legal prohibition and a moral counsel, the prohibition takes precedence. As between custom and law, there is little to choose between them when a conflict arises. One can as well argue that the one should have priority as that the other should.

It has also been noted not only how custom creates law, but also how law is abrogated by custom.

Both custom and law have their institutional aspects. I have suggested that for those customs which have sanctions attached to them, there are informal "courts of custom," whose procedures are less precise than those of the more formal courts of law, but whose effectiveness is beyond question. The International Court of Justice, the court of the bush, and the football team's "commission" all function with some degree of effectiveness. To the extent that they do, they are evidence for the existence of law.

There may be occasions when we will want to deny that one or another of these has legal power. If the "commission" had sentenced one of the boys to death, no doubt some higher authority would have declared that it lacked the legal capacity to do so. If the International Court of Justice renders a verdict which is unacceptable to one of the parties to a dispute, it is conceivable that the party might determine, unilaterally, that the decision goes "beyond" the law and is therefore invalid. These courts are feeble, but they do serve a function, and the function they serve is a legal one. Within their recognized capacities, they render verdicts that are accepted by certain people. To the extent that this is true, they are acting as agencies of law. But our courts and other legal agencies have their limitations as well. The ultimate criterion by which we determine whether X is a law is not the form X takes, nor its content, but its effectiveness, the extent to which it facilitates the orderly settlement of disputes and regulates the lives of those who are under its jurisdiction. Whatever the content of X may be, whatever its forms, when it ceases to be effective, it is no law.

None of this emphasis on judicial institutions should be construed to mean that I am substituting a new kind of legal realism for the old, or that I am propounding a new, expanded conception of judges and courts. But I am suggesting that for some important purposes, we must be prepared to broaden our conceptions of these terms. I am urging the view that neither formal nor informal courts are necessary for the existence of law, and have tried to show, through a number of examples, how law can exist where there are no courts of any kind, just as certain forms of custom can exist in the absence of sanctions.

It is not the formality with which a court conducts its business that determines whether it is a court of law. It is its effectiveness. Some highly formal legal institutions are relatively ineffectual, and some rather informal ones are quite effective. And finally, there are some systems of law that work in the complete absence of formal legal institutions and means of imposing sanctions. Certain voluntary religious organizations might be cited as examples.

What, then, is the relation of custom to law? It depends on what we mean by "custom" and by "law." In certain senses, "custom" and "law" are identical; neither can be distinguished from the other. For some purposes, it is useful to formulate certain technical distinctions, confining the term "law," for example, to that which is enforced in the courts, and "custom" to those regular forms of behavior which are variously denominated rules of etiquette, rituals, practices, regulations, and the like, but which are not enforced by the courts. Under this definition, "custom" and "law" are not identical, but they exert powerful influences upon one another, "custom" causing judges to make decisions which they might otherwise not make and bringing legislators to pass laws which they might otherwise not pass, and "law" causing people to revise their practices. In those areas where "custom" is accompanied by sanctions, it is determinative of rights and duties, powers and liabilities and disabilities; and the same is true of law. For some purposes, it is useful to be able to distinguish between those rights and duties (and the rest) that are enforceable in the courts and those that are not. Once a given customary "right" becomes widely accepted, it may be sanctioned by the courts as well, even without the relevant formal legislation, and in this way, custom becomes a source of law.

The inquiry into this subject has just begun. Much remains to be done. In particular, the relations between custom and morality remain virtually untouched. To what extent and in what senses does custom serve as a source of morals? What are the effects of moral prescriptions upon customs? What are (or ought to be) their relations? To what extent does desuetude bring about changes in moral standards, and to what extent ought it to do so? These are only a few of the questions for future investigation suggested by analogy with the present study.

Appendix A

Table of Customs

The table following schematizes the findings on most of the kinds of "custom" discussed in Chapter I. Each type is named; the name is followed by a series of numbers which are either plain numerals or qualified. Those which are qualified are either preceded by a negative sign or enclosed in parentheses. The negative sign indicates that the attribute opposite to that designated by the positive number applies to that type of custom. The parentheses indicate that that attribute is not relevant to that type of custom, or for some reason cannot be found in that type of custom. An asterisk indicates that the terms used in that instance have a unique characteristic not found in other instances of the same terms.

For simplicity's sake, all the designations are spelled out below:

1. S regularly does X. ~1. S does not regularly do X.

2. S might choose not to do X, and not do X. ~2. S is either unable to choose not to do X, or is under some compulsion to do X.

3. S is conscious of doing X. ~3. S is not conscious of doing X. (3) Whether S is conscious of doing X or not is irrelevant.

4. S does X deliberately. ~4. S does not do X deliber-

ately. (4) Whether S does X deliberately or not is irrelevant.

5. S believes he ought to do X. ~5. S believes he ought
not to do X. (5) S's belief as to his obligation to do or to
refrain from doing X is irrelevant. *Or* S believes that he
is permitted to do either X or ~X.

6. If S fails to do X, he is subject to sanctions. ~6. If
S fails to do X, he is not subject to sanctions. (6) Whether
S is subject to sanctions for doing X is irrelevant. *Or* he
may or may not be subject to sanctions.

7. S may be prevented from violating the rule to do
X by the group or its representative. ~7. S may not be
prevented from violating the rule to do X by the group or
its representative. (7) Whether the group may prevent S
from doing X is irrelevant (or there is no such group).

8. The group may suspend or abolish the rule that X
is to be done. ~8. The group may not suspend or abolish
the rule that X is to be done. (8) Whether the group may
suspend or abolish the rule that X is to be performed is
irrelevant (or there is no such group).

9. S does X with special intent (*kavvanah*). ~9. S does
not do X with special intent. (9) Whether S does X with
special intent is irrelevant.

Habit: 1, 2, ~3, ~4, ~5, (6), (7), (8), ~9
Maxim: 1, 2, 3, 4, 5, ~6, ~7, (8), (9)
Practice: 1, 2, 3, 4, (5), ~6, ~7, 8, (9)
Regulation: 1, 2, 3, (4), 5, 6, 7, 8, (9)
Style: 1, 2, (3), (4), (5), (6), (7), (8), (9)
Etiquette: 1, 2, (3), (4), (5), 6, ~7, 8, (9)
Ritual: 1, 2, 3, 4, 5, 6, 7, 8, 9
Constitutive Rules: 1*, ~2*, 3, 4, (5), 6*, 7*, 8, (9)
Simple custom: 1, 2, (3), (4), (5), 6, ~7, ~8, (9)

Appendix B

Some Other Positivists

Spinoza takes a strongly Hobbesian point of view in his political philosophy, for he too conceives of the state of nature as a *bellum omnium contra omnes,*[1] and he also agrees that the supreme authorities (*viz.,* those who wield the greatest power) are the only persons who "have the right of deciding what is good, evil, equitable, or iniquitous, that is, what must be done or left undone by the subjects severally or collectively. And, accordingly, we say that they have the sole right of laying down laws, and of interpreting the same, whenever their meaning is disputed."[2] But the commonwealth itself is bound by no law but the law of nature, which is vindicated only by war; and it is bound even to the laws of nature only in the sense that it must observe certain rules or precepts in order to assure it independence.[3]

Therefore, just as for Hobbes no custom assumes the status of law simply by virtue of its long status as usage of the people, so also for Spinoza the consent of the sovereign is necessary, and his decree is sufficient to ban any observance, no matter how long it may have stood.

[1] *Tractatus Politicus,* Chapter iii, Sec. 13 *et seq.*
[2] Ibid., Chapter iv, Sec. 1. Tr. by R. H. M. Elwes, Bohn's Philosophical Library (London: G. Bell & Sons, 1917), Vol. II, 309. See also Chapter iii, Secs. 3–5.
[3] Ibid., Chapter iv, Sec. 5, 311.

And just as Hobbes's theory of the nature of law as the command of a sovereign power logically implies that between nations who have not yet set up such a sovereign power there is no true law; so also for Spinoza there is no true international law.[4]

Since each commonwealth is in a state of nature relative to each other commonwealth, it follows that "a commonwealth . . . is so far independent, as it can plan and provide against oppression by another, and so far dependent on another commonwealth, as it fears that other's power, or is hindered by it from executing its own wishes, or lastly, as it needs its help for its own preservation or increase."[5] Since the nations are in a continual state of war with one another (in the Hobbesian sense of being in a state of nature), if one nation desires to wage war upon another, it may "lawfully" do so, even if its only purpose is "to make that other dependent on itself."[6] Even when two nations have contracted with one another (through pact or treaty), such contracts are valid only so long as the motives for entering into them subsist. But the moment such motives are removed, the contract "breaks of itself," and therefore "every commonwealth has the right to break its contract, whenever it chooses, and cannot be said to act treacherously or perfidiously in breaking its word. . . ." If the other party to the contract complains that it has been deceived, Spinoza says, it should not blame the bad faith of the other commonwealth, "but its own folly in having entrusted its own welfare to another party, that was independent, and had for its highest law the welfare of its own dominion."[7] Where occasion demands, there is nothing at all wrong with the supreme authority breaking its word.[8]

[4] Ibid., Chapter iii, Sec. 11, 306.
[5] Ibid., Sec. 12, 306.
[6] Ibid., Sec. 13, 307.
[7] Ibid., Sec. 14, 307. See also Secs. 15–18.
[8] Ibid., Sec. 17, 308. Cf. also *Tractatus Theologico-Politicus,* Elwes edition, xviff. (See n. 3 above for details.)

It follows, then, that "contracts" between sovereign states are not contracts in any proper sense at all, for they are good only so long as the "contracting" parties care to abide by them. If even treaties and other written agreements between nations have no binding legal validity, then surely custom has none. Thus, according to Spinoza, custom is neither identical with nor in any sense a source of international law, since there is no international law properly so called; and though it may be a source of civil law, it is so only at the pleasure of the sovereign.

Samuel Pufendorf is also in the Hobbesian tradition. His *De Jure Naturae et Gentium, Libri Octo* reveals the influence of Hobbes throughout. As regards the question currently under discussion, there is no doubt that he follows the doctrine of Hobbes. He quotes *De Cive* (Chapter xiv, Secs. 4–5) with approval, agreeing with Hobbes's doctrine that the natural law, when applied to whole states or nations or peoples, is called the law of nations.[9] He goes on:

> Nor do we feel that there is any voluntary or positive law of nations which has the force of law, properly so called, such as binds nations as if it proceeded from a superior. . . . And so we do not, as a matter of fact, disagree with those who like to define the law of nature as that which is in conformity with rational nature, and the law of nations as that which proceeds from considerations of our requirements which are helped most of all by sociable attitude; for we deny the existence of any law of nations arising from a superior. . . .[10]

What, then, shall we make of those long-established usages to which all civilized men have adhered? Particularly in warfare, certain customs are observed "by a certain tacit agreement" concerning the exemption of certain persons and things from the violence of war, the

[9] Pufendorf, *De Jure* . . . , tr. Oldfather (Washington: Carnegie Endowment), 226.
[10] Ibid.

treatment of captives, the kinds of weapons that may be used against enemies, and the like. Machiavelli, for example, relates how the mercenary armies in Italy refrained from shooting missiles into besieged cities at night, and how the garrisons likewise refrained from shooting missiles into the tents of the besieging armies. Strabo, too, tells of armies which agreed not to use missiles, and among the Hindus it was customary not to molest farmers during civil wars.

Pufendorf replies that we may make nothing of them. If a belligerent refuses to abide by such "agreements" or customs, "he may be accused of no fault other than a kind of ungentlemanliness."[11] One might prefer to observe such customs for certain advantages which they might entail—though Pufendorf is more inclined to think that those who engage in unjust wars are rather inclined to give fastidious attention to such details in order to give the appearance, at least, of being concerned with right and justice. However, the main point is simply that those obligations which rest upon tacit agreement are not strictly obligatory, and anyone who expressly declares that he will not be bound by them is not in fact bound by them at all. In this way, such customs become obsolete or abrogated by contrary customs.

> And there is no reason for any one to make complaints, as if this doctrine destroyed the safeguards of the security, interest, and safety of nations, since these surely lie not in such customs, but in the observance of the law of nature, which is much more sacred. If this latter be intact, mankind has no need whatsoever of the former.[12]

Like Hobbes, Pufendorf distinguishes carefully between law on the one hand and counsel and contract on the other; and the distinctions are virtually identical with those drawn by Hobbes.[13] The difference between a

11 Pufendorf, *De Jure . . .* , 228.
12 Ibid.
13 Ibid.

doctor urging his patient not to smoke and a lawgiver prohibiting the smoking of cigarettes is that in the one case the patient is free to follow his doctor's advice or not and the real ground for whatever obligation he may have to follow that advice is the soundness of the doctor's reasons for urging him not to smoke; while in the other case the subject is not free to ignore the prohibition if he so desires, and he has a true obligation laid upon him—not because of the soundness of the legislator's reasons for commanding him as he does, for the legislator may either have no truly sound reasons or he may not bother to make them known to his subjects, but simply because of the power he possesses to enforce obedience to his will.

As for the notion that laws are "common agreements" or contracts, Pufendorf points out first that by their very nature, neither natural laws nor divine positive laws originated in agreements among men. But leaving that aside, it is clear, he says, that even civil laws are not agreements or conventions for the most part. Even where men are truly free to enter into agreements or contracts, he says, as in a democracy, those who withhold their consent are not bound by the contract's provisions; while when a decree is enacted by the vote of the people, those who opposed the decree are bound by its provisions as well as those who favored it.

The major distinction between true agreements and laws, he says, lies in the fact that agreements originate in the will of the parties, and therefore no party to a prospective agreement is obligated to any other (insofar as the terms of that agreement are concerned) until after the agreement has been made and it has been determined what the parties are to do; laws, however, do not originate in the will of the persons who are expected to carry out their provisions, but in the will of the legislator, who is presumed to have the power to enforce the carrying out of those provisions, and therefore the persons to whom a prospective law applies are presumed to owe an obligation to the legislator *even before the law is enacted,* and the decree itself merely spells out what those persons must do in order to fulfill their obligations. In short, a law is defined by Pufendorf as

> a decree by which a superior obligates a subject to adapt his actions to the former's command. We use the term *decree,* not because it exists in the mind and will of the one who gives the decree, but because it is communicated to the subject in such a way that he recognizes he must bend himself to it, and on that account it is equivalent for us to a command.[14]

Again we are left with the conclusion that there is no true international law, so there can be no customary international law; and since law is a command coming down to the populace from those who wield authority, customs reflecting the will of the people do not *per se* have true obligations attached to them, and do not possess lawmaking capacities (or cannot serve as sources of law).

Many others have held similar views. Gierke[15] lists N. H. Gundling, J. N. Hertius, U. Huber, J. H. Boehmer, J. H. G. von Justi, and H. G. Scheidemantel.[16] Justi, for example, argues that nations are in a state of nature relative to one another, and that they are therefore neither subject to any laws which may be decreed by any higher tribunal (since there is none) nor bound by international agreements or customs (since there in no true international society). They are, however, subject to the so-called duties of good fellowship. And Scheidemantel, who holds that law is the declared will of majesty, states that custom, which generally arises through "culpable heedlessness or malice" and is most often a matter of willful disobedience, is invalid whenever it is in opposition to law.

These, then, are a few representatives of the positivist position criticized above.

14 Pufendorf, *De Jure,* 89.
15 Otto Gierke, *Natural Law and the Theory of Society: 1500 to 1800,* tr. by Sir Ernest Barker (Boston: Beacon Press, 1957).
16 Ibid., 168, 373, n. 30.

Appendix C

The Relation of the Written Law to Custom

Our discussion of the relation between custom and law would not be complete, technically, without some consideration of certain minor points, such as the relation of writing to custom, the amount of time that must elapse between the adoption of a practice and its becoming a custom in the fullest sense of the word, and so on. These, I say, are minor points, for the questions they raise are trivial. It is obvious, from what we have said, that reducing a custom to writing will make little or no difference to its continued existence. Those who have a narrow conception of law may say that once a custom is reduced to writing and thereby becomes enforceable in courts of law (for example), it ceases to be a custom. This only shows that they have not only a narrow conception of law, but a narrow conception of custom as well. Enforcing a custom in a court of law does not remove it from the realm of custom. Rather, to whatever customary sanctions there may be, it adds one more sanction, which is applied —if it is applied at all—in a more rigidly formalized way. The practice does not cease to be a custom on the day it is enacted into law. I would say rather that the converse is more likely to be true: that on the day it ceases to be a custom, it ceases to be a law.

CUSTOM AND TEMPORAL LIMITATIONS

All temporal specifications, setting minimum times during which people must engage in a given form of activity before it becomes a custom, are arbitrary and meaningless. Suárez sets ten years as the minimum time required for the establishment of a custom. Why this period of time should be superior to fifteen years, five generations, or five years is nowhere made clear. In law courts, where people like to pretend that everything is clear and precise, certain arbitrary limits are set—but then no one seriously tries to prove that a custom dates back to 1215 or whatever the date may be; resort is had to fictions instead. The vague and imprecise term "immemorial antiquity" at least has the virtue of permitting the judges enough leeway to allow them to retain their integrity when deciding whether a given practice is a custom or not. For the boys in my story, the custom of submitting disputes to the "commission" is already of immemorial antiquity, though the narrator remembers a time when it did not exist.

Bibliography

The books and articles listed below constitute a large portion of the sources used in preparation of this study. However, the list is not exhaustive. No attempt has been made to separate those works which are cited directly in the body of this study from those which are not. The reader can glean that information from the footnotes.

ALLEN, J. W., *A History of Political Thought in the Sixteenth Century*. New York: Barnes & Noble, 1928.

AQUINAS, ST. THOMAS, *Summa Theologica,* translated by the Dominican Fathers, in Anton C. Pegis, *Basic Writings of Saint Thomas Aquinas.*

AUSTIN, JOHN, *The Province of Jurisprudence Determined,* with introduction by H. L. A. Hart. London: Weidenfeld and Nicholson, 1954.

AYER, A. J., "The Principle of Utility," in G. W. Keeton (ed.), *Jeremy Bentham and the Law.* London: Stevens, 1948.

BAIER, KURT, *The Moral Point of View.* Ithaca, New York: Cornell University Press, 1958.

BARKER, SIR ERNEST, *Greek Political Theory, Plato and His Predecessors.* London: Methuen, 1918.

BARKER, SIR ERNEST, *The Political Thought of Plato and Aristotle.* New York: Dover Publications, 1959.

BARKER, SIR ERNEST, *The Politics of Aristotle*. Oxford: Oxford University Press, 1948.

BARKUN, MICHAEL, *Law without Sanctions*. New Haven: Yale University Press, 1968.

BECK, LEWIS WHITE, *Commentary on Kant's Critique of Practical Reason*. Chicago: University of Chicago Press, 1960.

BENTHAM, JEREMY, *A Fragment on Government and an Introduction to the Principles of Morals and Legislation*. Oxford: Basil Blackwell, 1960.

————, *The Limits of Jurisprudence Defined*. New York: Columbia University Press, 1945.

BLACKSTONE, WILLIAM B., *Commentaries on the Laws of England*. Boston: Beacon Press, 1962.

BOORSTIN, DANIEL J., *The Mysterious Science of Law*. Boston: Beacon Press, 1941.

BRANDT, RICHARD, *Ethical Theory*. Englewood Cliffs, New Jersey: Prentice-Hall, 1959.

BRANDT, RICHARD B., (ed.), *Social Justice*. Englewood Cliffs, New Jersey: Prentice-Hall, 1962.

BREDVOLD, LOUIS and ROSS, RALPH, *The Philosophy of Edmund Burke*. Ann Arbor: University of Michigan Press, 1960.

BRIERLY, J. L., *The Law of Nations*, Sixth Ed. Oxford: Oxford University Press, 1963.

BRINTON, CRANE, *English Political Thought in the 19th Century*. New York: Harper & Row, 1962.

BROWN, BRENDAN F., *The Natural Law Reader*. New York: Oceana Publications, 1960.

BRYCE, JAMES, *Studies in History and Jurisprudence*. London: Oxford University Press, 1901.

BUCHANAN, SCOTT, *Rediscovering Natural Law*. Santa Barbara, California: Center for the Study of Democratic Institutions, 1962.

CAHN, EDMOND N., *The Sense of Injustice*. New York: New York University Press, 1949.

CASSIRER, ERNST, *The Myth of the State*. New Haven: Yale University Press, 1949.

CASSUTO, UMBERTO, *Perush 'al Sefer Shemot*, Second Ed. Jerusalem: Hebrew University Press, 1953.

CASTAÑEDA, HECTOR-NERI, *et al.*, *Morality and the Lan-*

guage of Conduct. Detroit: Wayne State University Press, 1963.

CHAMBLISS, ROLLIN, *Social Thought.* New York: Holt, Rinehart & Winston, 1954.

COHEN, CARL, *Communism, Fascism and Democracy.* New York: Random House, 1962.

COHEN, FELIX S., *Ethical Systems and Legal Ideals.* New York: Great Seal Books, 1933.

DAHL, ROBERTS A., *A Preface to Democratic Theory.* Chicago: University of Chicago Press, 1956.

DAVIS, PHILIP E., *Moral Duty and Legal Responsibility.* New York: Appleton-Century-Crofts, 1966.

DE JOUVENAL, BERTRAND, *Power.* London: Batchworth Press, 1945.

D'ENTRÈVES, A. P., *Natural Law: An Introduction to Legal Philosophy.* London: Hutchinson University Library, 1951.

DRIVER, G. R., and JOHN C. MILES, *The Babylonian Laws.* Oxford: Oxford University Press, 1960.

DUPRE, LOUIS, *The Philosophical Foundations of Marxism.* New York: Harcourt, Brace & World, 1966.

EBENSTEIN, WILLIAM, *Great Political Thinkers.* New York: Holt, Rinehart & Winston, 1965.

EHRLICH, EUGEN, *Fundamental Principles of the Sociology of Law.* Cambridge, Massachusetts: Harvard University Press, 1936.

FOSTER, MICHAEL B., *Masters of Political Thought.* Boston: Houghton Mifflin, 1941.

FRANK, JEROME, *Law and the Modern Mind.* New York: Doubleday, 1930.

FRANKEL, JOSEPH, *International Relations.* New York: Oxford University Press, 1964.

FRIEDRICH, CARL JOACHIM, *The Philosophy of Law in Historical Perspective.* Chicago: University of Chicago Press, 1958.

FULLER, LON L., *The Morality of Law.* New Haven: Yale University Press, 1964.

———, "Positivism and Fidelity to Law: A Reply to Professor Hart." In Olafson, see below.

GARLAN, EDWIN NORMAN, *Legal Realism and Justice.* New York: Columbia University Press, 1941.

GEWIRTH, ALAN, *Political Philosophy.* Chicago: University of Chicago Press, 1941.

GIERKE, OTTO, *Natural Law and the Theory of Society: 1500 to 1800,* tr. by Sir Ernest Barker. Boston: Beacon Press, 1957.

HARDING, ALAN, *The Social History of English Law.* Baltimore: Penguin Books, 1966.

HART, H. L. A., *The Concept of Law.* Oxford: Oxford University Press, 1961.

————, *Law, Liberty, and Morality.* London: Oxford University Press, 1963.

————, "Positivism and the Separation of Law and Morals," *Harvard Law Review* (1958), reprinted in F. A. Olafson, *Society, Law, and Morality.* Englewood Cliffs, New Jersey: Prentice-Hall, 1961.

————, and HONORE, A. M., *Causation in the Law.* Oxford: Clarendon Press, 1959.

HENSON, RAY D., *Landmarks of Law.* Boston: Beacon Press, 1960.

HOBBES, THOMAS, *De Cive,* Sterling P. Lamprecht (ed.). New York: Appleton-Century-Crofts, 1949.

————, *Leviathan.* New York: Library of Liberal Arts, 1958.

HOEBEL, E. ADAMSON, *The Law of Primitive Man.* Cambridge, Massachusetts: Harvard University Press, 1964.

HOHFELD, W. N., *Fundamental Legal Conceptions.* First printed in 1913. Reprinted by Yale University Press, New Haven, 1964.

HOOK, SIDNEY, *Law and Philosophy: A Symposium.* New York: New York University Press, 1964.

JENSEN, O. C., *The Nature of Legal Argument.* Oxford: Basil Blackwell, 1957.

JONES, J. WALTER, *The Law and Legal Theory of the Greeks.* Oxford: Oxford University Press, 1956.

KANTOROWICZ, HERMANN, *The Definition of Law.* Cambridge: Cambridge University Press, 1958.

KAUFMANN, YEHEZKEL, *Toledot Ha-emunah Ha-yisraelit,* Sixth Ed., 4 vols. Jerusalem and Tel Aviv: Mosad Bialik and Dvir, 1964.

KELSEN, HANS, *General Theory of Law and State,* tr. A. Wedberg. New York: Russell & Russell, 1961.

————, *What Is Justice?* Berkeley: University of California Press, 1960.

LADD, JOHN, "Custom," in *The Encyclopedia of Philoso-*

phy, Vol. II, Paul Edwards (ed.). New York: Macmillan, 1967.

————, *The Structure of a Moral Code.* Cambridge, Massachusetts: Harvard University Press, 1957.

LASKI, H. J., *Political Thought in England.* London: Oxford University Press, 1920.

LAUTERPACHT, H., *Oppenheim's International Law,* Seventh Ed. London: Longmans, Green, 1948.

LERNER, RALPH, and MUHDIN MAHDI, *Medieval Political Philosophy.* Glencoe, Illinois: Free Press, 1963.

LEVI, EDWARD H., *An Introduction to Legal Reasoning.* Chicago: University of Chicago Press, 1948.

LOCKE, JOHN, *Essays on the Law of Nature,* tr. and ed. by W. Van Leyden. Oxford: Oxford University Press, 1958.

LUCAS, J. R., *The Principles of Politics.* Oxford: Oxford University Press, 1966.

MCILWAIN, C. H., *The Growth of Political Thought in the West.* New York: Macmillan, 1932.

MALINOWSKI, B., Introduction to H. I. Hogbin's *Law and Order in Polynesia.* Hamden, Connecticut: Shoe String Press, 1961, reprint of 1934 ed.

MAYO, BERNARD, *Ethics and the Moral Life.* London: Macmillan, 1958.

MOORE, B., *Political Power and Social Theory.* New York: Harper & Brothers, 1958.

MORRALL, J. B., *Political Thought in Medieval Times.* New York: Harper & Brothers, 1958.

NEGLEY, GLENN, *Political Authority and Moral Judgment.* Durham, North Carolina: Duke University Press, 1965.

OLAFSON, FREDERICK A., *Justice and Social Policy.* Englewood Cliffs, New Jersey: Prentice-Hall, 1961.

OLIVECRONA, KARL, *Law As Fact.* Copenhagen: Einar Munksgaard, 1939.

OPPENHEIM, L., *International Law: A Treatise.* New York: Longmans, Green, 1952.

PARRY, CLIVE, *The Sources and Evidences of International Law.* New York: Oceana Publications, 1965.

PERELMAN, C., *The Idea of Justice and the Problem of Argument.* New York: Humanities Press, 1963.

————, *Justice.* New York: Random House, 1967.

PLAMENATZ, JOHN, *Man and Society*. New York: Mc-
Graw-Hill, 1963.

POPPER, KARL R., *The Open Society and Its Enemies*.
London: Routledge & Kegan Paul, 1962.

POUND, ROSCOE, *An Introduction to the Philosophy of Law*.
New Haven: Yale University Press, 1922.

PUCHTA, GEORG F., *Das Gewohnheitsrecht*. Erlangen:
Palmsche Verlagsbuch, 1837.

PUFENDORF, SAMUEL, *De Jure Natura et Jus Gentium,
Libri Octo,* tr. C. H. and W. A. Oldfather. Washington: Carnegie Endowment for International Peace,
1934.

QUINTON, ANTHONY, *Political Philosophy*. Oxford: Oxford
University Press, 1967.

RADCLIFF, PETER, *Limits of Liberty*. Belmont, California:
Wadsworth, 1966.

RAPHAEL, D. D., (ed.), *Political Theory and the Rights of
Man*. Bloomington: Indiana University Press, 1965.

SEAGLE, WILLIAM, *The History of Law*. First published as
The Quest for Law, in 1941. New York: Knopf,
1946.

SHUMAN, SAMUEL I., *Legal Positivism*. Detroit: Wayne
State University Press, 1963.

SPINOZA, *Works,* tr. by R. H. M. Elwes. London: G.
Bell & Sons, 1912.

STANKIEWICZ, W. F., *Political Thought Since World War
II*. London: Collier-Macmillan, 1964.

STANLIS, PETER J., *Edmund Burke and the Natural Law*.
Ann Arbor: University of Michigan Press, 1958.

STONE, JULIUS, *Legal System and Lawyers' Reasonings*.
Stanford California: Stanford University Press,
1964.

————, *Province and Function of Law*. Sydney, Aus-
tralia: Associated General Publications, 1946.

STRAUSS, LEO, *Natural Right and History*. Chicago: University of Chicago Press, 1953.

STUMPE, S. E., *Morality and the Law*. Nashville, Tennes-
see: Vanderbilt University Press, 1966.

SUÁREZ, FRANCISCO, *Treatise on Laws and God the Law-
giver (De Legibus, ac Deo Legislatore)*, 1612. Published by the Carnegie Endowment for International
Peace in the Classics of International Law series,

with translation. London: Oxford University Press, 1944.

TAYLOR, JOHN F. A., *The Masks of Society,* New York: Appleton-Century-Crofts, 1966.

TAYLOR, PAUL W., *Problems of Moral Philosophy*. Belmont, California: Dickenson, 1967.

ULLMAN, WALTER, *A History of Political Thought: The Middle Ages*. Baltimore: Penguin Books, 1965.

WARNOCK, MARY, *Ethics Since 1900*. London: Oxford University Press, 1960.

WELDON, T. D., *The Vocabulary of Politics*. Baltimore: Penguin Books, 1953.

WITTGENSTEIN, LUDWIG, *Philosophical Investigations,* tr. G. E. M. Anscombe. Oxford: Basil Blackwell, 1958.

WOLFF, ROBERT PAUL, *Political Man and Social Man*. New York: Random House, 1966.

Index